SQL Server Secret Diary

Know the unknown secrets of SQL Server

For SQL Server 2005 and 2008

Vijayan J

MK.Krizh

Copyright

This book is dedicated to our parents, friends and to the readers.

Preface

This book is made for developers who already know SQL Server and want to gain more knowledge in SQL Server. This book is not for starters who want to start from the beginning.

The problem-solution approach will help you to understand and solve the real-time problems easily.

This Book will teach you

- How to solve common real-time problems.
- How to improve performance.
- How to protect your data and code.
- How to reduce your code.
- How to use SQL Server efficiently.
- Advanced topics with simple examples.
- Tips and tricks with sample queries.
- And also teach how to do in the better way.

We promise you, this book definitely teaches you something which you never learnt from any other books and increase your self-rating in SQL Server.

This book applies to **SQL Server 2005 and 2008** and all the solutions are tested with both versions.

Contents

1. How to secure source code of stored procedure, UDF and view?

If we create database object using "WITH ENCRYPTION" option, nobody can view the source code of the database object either using SP_HELPTEXT or SQL Server Management Studio (SSMS). The database objects can be a stored procedure, user defined function (UDF) and View.

If we try to view the source code, the SQL Server throws an error.

Syntax:

```
CREATE PROCEDURE <Stored Procedure Name>

WITH ENCRYPTION

AS

        -- Stored procedure logic comes here
```

Example:

```
CREATE PROCEDURE Country_SelectAll

WITH ENCRYPTION

AS

        SELECT code,name FROM Country

GO
```

Above example creates a stored procedure with WITH ENCRYPTION option.

Example:

```
sp_helptext 'Country_SelectAll'
```

Trying to view the stored procedure created with WITH ENCRYPTION option.

Output:

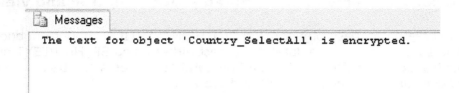

Caution:

While creating database objects, using WITH ENCRYPTION option, we have to keep actual source code as files otherwise we cannot get the source code. We recommend using version control to keep the source code of all database objects.

2. How to use GO statement in SQL Server?

Go statement is used to separate SQL statements into independent batches. Every batch uses different execution plans.

When SQL Server finds errors while parsing a query batch, it throws error and does not execute any queries in the batch.

When "GO" statement is used in the query batch, statements are considered as different batches.

Example A:

```
USE Demo

DELETE * FROM Country -- This statement will throw error, because
* is invalid in DELETE

SELECT * FROM Country
```

Output:

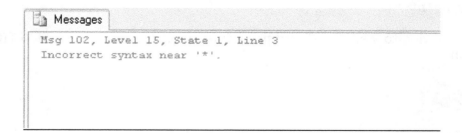

Example B:

```
USE Demo

GO

DELETE * FROM Country -- This statement will throw error, because
* is invalid in DELETE

GO

SELECT * FROM Country
```

Output:

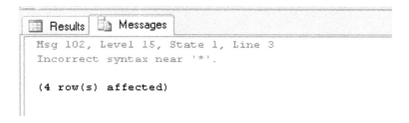

In this above example, even if the first query throws an error, the second query executed successfully because of "GO" statement. It separates two statements as two batches.

Example C:

```
CREATE DATABASE NewDB

USE NewDB

-- query batch to create objects in newDB
```

Output:

```
Messages
Msg 911, Level 16, State 1, Line 3
Could not locate entry in sysdatabases for database 'newDB'.
No entry found with that name. Make sure that the
name is entered correctly.
```

SQL Server parses whole statement and throwing error because *newDB* database does not exist.

Example D:

```
CREATE DATABASE NewBDB

GO

USE NewDB

-- query batch to create objects in NewDB
```

Output:

```
Messages
Command(s) completed successfully.
```

After adding GO statement the above query is working.

Example E:

```
USE Demo

CREATE   PROCEDURE #tmp_sp1

AS

BEGIN

     SELECT 'This is #tmp_sp1'

END

  --Creating #tmp_sp2

CREATE   PROCEDURE #tmp_sp2

AS

BEGIN

     SELECT 'This is #tmp_sp2'

END
```

Output:

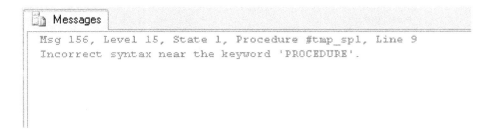

Here two CREATE statements are not separated by GO statement.

Example F:

```
USE Demo

CREATE   PROCEDURE #tmp_sp1

AS

BEGIN

     SELECT 'This is #tmp_sp1'

END

GO

  --Creating #tmp_sp2

CREATE   PROCEDURE #tmp_sp2

AS

BEGIN

     SELECT 'This is #tmp_sp2'

END
```

Output:

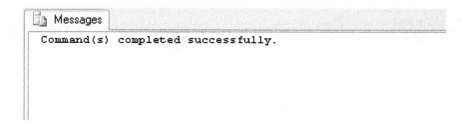

After adding GO statement the above query is working.

Note

Variables that are declared before the GO statement could not be used after the GO statement due to scope of batch.

3. How to repeat the statements without using loops?

GO <N> statement can be used to repeat the statements for N number of times.

Syntax:

```
BEGIN

    <SQL Statements>

END

GO <Number Of Executions>
```

Example A:

Following query executes 5 times.

```
USE Demo

SELECT * FROM Country

GO 5
```

Output:

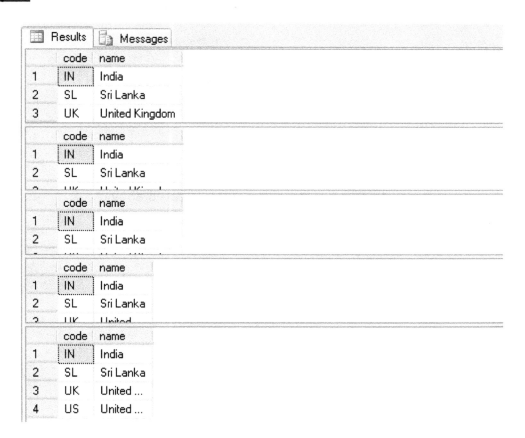

Example B:

Following query creates a temporary table for demonstration.

```
USE Demo

CREATE TABLE #Sample

        (

                RowID INT NOT NULL IDENTITY(1,1) ,

                j CHAR(3)

        )
GO
```

Following query inserts the values to the *#Sample* table 200 times using GO 200 statement.

```
BEGIN

INSERT INTO #Sample (j) VALUES ('ABC')

END

GO 200

SELECT * FROM #Sample
```

Following query deletes the temporary table created above.

```
GO

DROP TABLE #Sample

GO
```

Output:

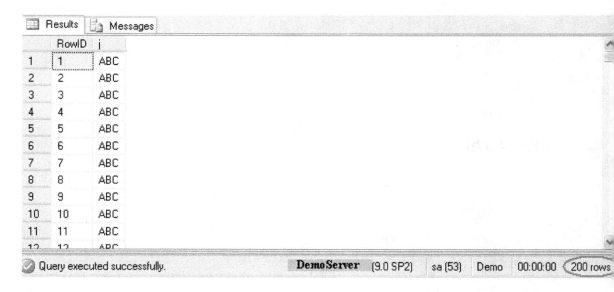

Note:

GO is a client command and not a T-SQL command. So GO or GO <N> can only be used with Microsoft SQL Server client tools. This GO <N> is mostly used to insert test data.

4. How to check the queries are ANSI compatible?

If we want to write generic queries, use FIPS_FLAGGER flag. It gives warning when the queries are not ANSI compatible.

Syntax:

```
-- To enable ANSI compatibility check
SET FIPS_FLAGGER '<<Level>>'
--Level value can be FULL or ENTRY or INTERMEDIATE
--To disable ANSI compatibility check
SET FIPS_FLAGGER OFF
```

Example A:

```
SET FIPS_FLAGGER 'FULL'

SELECT TOP 5 * FROM dbo.Country
```

Output:

```
Results   Messages

 FIPS Warning: Line 3 has the non-ANSI statement 'SET'.
 FIPS Warning: Line 4 has the non-ANSI clause 'TOP'.

 (4 row(s) affected)
```

Here SQL Server shows warning messages, because SET and TOP are not ANSI compatible.

Example B:

```
SET FIPS_FLAGGER OFF

SELECT TOP 5 * FROM dbo.Country
```

Once we disable the FIPS_FLAGGER flag, SQL Server stops showing ANSI compatible warnings.

Where to Use:

This option is necessary when we want to use the same queries in different database systems, for example, to run same queries in SQL Server and Oracle. Some of the SQL Server's T-SQL features may not be available in other database systems such as Oracle. But if the queries are ANSI compatible, it can run on almost all the database systems.

5. How to use ORDER BY clause in view?

As per RDBMS rule ORDER BY clause is not allowed in view. If we try to create ORDER BY clause in view, SQL Server throws error message.

The ORDER BY clause is invalid in view, inline functions, derived tables, and sub queries unless TOP is specified.

If we use TOP 100 PERCENT then it is possible to use the order by clause in view.

Syntax:

```
SELECT TOP 100 PERCENT <<Field(s)>> FROM <<Table (s)>>
ORDER BY <<Field(s)>>
```

Example A:

```
USE Demo

GO

CREATE VIEW vw_Country

AS

    SELECT * FROM dbo.Country ORDER BY Name
```

Output

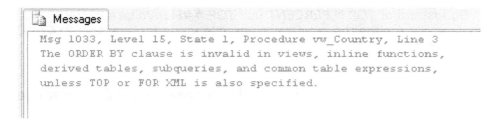

```
Msg 1033, Level 15, State 1, Procedure vw_Country, Line 3
The ORDER BY clause is invalid in views, inline functions,
derived tables, subqueries, and common table expressions,
unless TOP or FOR XML is also specified.
```

Example B:

The following example will execute successfully after adding the TOP clause.

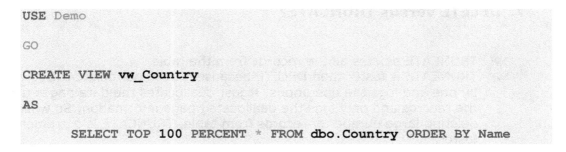

```
USE Demo

GO

CREATE VIEW vw_Country

AS

        SELECT TOP 100 PERCENT * FROM dbo.Country ORDER BY Name
```

Output

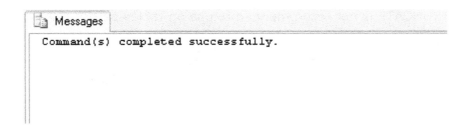

```
Command(s) completed successfully.
```

Note:

- SQL Server 2005 RTM has a bug that ignores the order by clause in view. Install the latest service pack to fix this bug. The above example query is working fine with service pack 2.
- SQL Server 2008 ignores ORDER BY DESC in views while used with TOP *N* PERCENT.

<u>Workaround:</u>

So instead of TOP N PERCENT use TOP ##MaxValue##. Here ##MaxValue## means the maximum possible value for example 2147483647, 10000000, etc...

6. How to use COUNT() function if the total records are larger than INT data type?

If the total rows are larger than INT data value (larger than 2,147,483,647), then use the COUNT_BIG() function instead of COUNT(),
This function use BIGINT data type and can support up to 2E63 −1 (9,223,372,036,854,775,807).

7. DELETE versus TRUNCATE?

- ➤ TRUNCATE deletes all the records from the table.
- ➤ TRUNCATE is faster than DELETE because it does not delete the rows one by one and logs the operations. It just deallocates the data pages used by the records and only logs the deallocated page information. So while deleting large number of records from table, TRUNCATE is extremely faster.
- ➤ TRUNCATE does not support WHERE clause.
- ➤ TRUNCATE does not update statistics.
- ➤ TRUNCATE does not work on the table referenced by foreign key.
- ➤ TRUNCATE reseeds the identity column value to initial value.
- ➤ While truncating table, trigger does not fire.
- ➤ TRUNCATE is not recommended to use on tables participating in indexed views.
- ➤ TRUNCATE does not affect the structure of table.
- ➤ After using TRUNCATE also we can rollback data.
- ➤ DELETE is classified as DML and TRUNCATE is classified as DDL.

<u>Syntax:</u>

```
TRUNCATE TABLE <<Table name>>
```

8. What is the recommended way to get the list of database objects?

Most of the developers use *sysobjects* system table to query the list of database objects, but Microsoft does not recommend querying *sysobjects* system tables and all the undocumented system databases objects.

Microsoft recommends using the *information_schema* prefixed views or documented stored procedures.

To get information about table

Syntax:

```
SELECT * FROM information_schema.tables  WHERE table_name
='<Table name>'
```

Example:

```
USE Demo

SELECT * FROM information_schema.tables
```

Output:

	TABLE_CATALOG	TABLE_SCHEMA	TABLE_NAME	TABLE_TYPE
1	DEMO	dbo	Rdbms	BASE TABLE
2	DEMO	dbo	User_Audit	BASE TABLE
3	DEMO	dbo	Vew_Labor_Rule1	VIEW
4	DEMO	dbo	Country	BASE TABLE
5	DEMO	dbo	Tbl_Sample	BASE TABLE
6	DEMO	dbo	Identity_Test	BASE TABLE
7	DEMO	dbo	Identity_Test2	BASE TABLE

To get information about view

Syntax:

```
SELECT * FROM information_schema.views WHERE table_name='<view
name>'
```

Example:

```
USE Demo

SELECT * FROM information_schema.views
```

Output:

	TABLE_CATA...	TABLE_SC...	TABLE_N...	VIEW_DEFINITION	CHECK_OPTI...	IS_UPDATABLE
1	Demo	dbo	vw_Country	CREATE VIEW vw_Country AS ...	NONE	NO

To get information about column

Syntax:

```
SELECT * FROM information_schema.columns WHERE table_name
='<Table name>'
```

Example:

```
USE Demo

SELECT * FROM information_schema.columns WHERE table_name
='Country'
```

Output:

	TABLE_CATALOG	TABLE_SCHEMA	TABLE_NAME	COLUMN_NAME	ORDINAL_POSITI
1	Demo	dbo	Country	code	1
2	Demo	dbo	Country	name	2

Recommended system stored procedures

- SP_HELP – Lists all the database objects from the current database without parameter.
- SP_Help '<database object name>' returns the detailed information about the database object.
- SP_Tables – Lists all the tables and views from the current database.

- SP_stored_procedures– Lists all the stored procedures from the current database.

9. SET Versus SELECT?

- SET can assign one variable at a time but SELECT can able to do multiple assignments.
- SET is the ANSI standard for assigning variables.
- If we use SELECT keyword for multiple assignments, it will boost your performance.

Example A (using SET):

```
USE Demo

GO

DECLARE @employeeid INT

DECLARE @tot INT

DECLARE @a INT

SET @employeeid = 1

SET @tot = 3000000



WHILE @employeeid < @tot

BEGIN

    SET @employeeid = @employeeid + 1

    SET  @a = 2

END

PRINT @employeeid
```

Output:

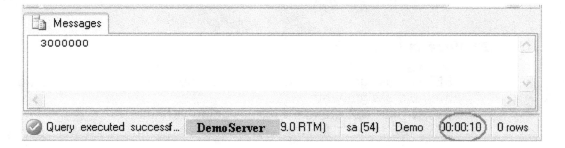

Example B (using SELECT):

```
USE Demo

GO

DECLARE @employeeid INT

DECLARE @tot INT

DECLARE @a INT

SET @employeeid = 1

SET @tot = 3000000

WHILE @employeeid < @tot

BEGIN

    SELECT @employeeid = @employeeid + 1,@a = 2

END

PRINT @employeeid
```

Output:

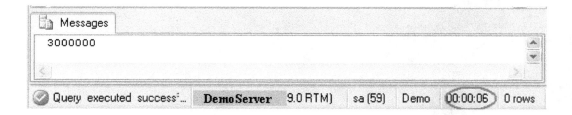

When executing these both queries we can find Example B(SELECT) performance is three times faster than SET. SELECT improves performance during multiple assignments.

While doing single assignment, there is no difference in performance.

Note:

Time taken to execute the above example may vary based on machine configuration. To increase the test cycles, we need to increase the variable *@tot*.

10.   How to do case sensitive searches in SQL Server?

Convert CHAR/VARCHAR datatypes to BINARY/VARBINARY datatypes and then compare. After the conversion, all the characters are represented as binary values. In binary representation lowercase and uppercase characters have different values so the comparison is case sensitive.

The following example filters the *password* column with the value 'IloveSQL' in all possible cases.

Example A:

```
USE Demo

SELECT      * FROM      dbo.Users WHERE    userName = 'James' AND
password = 'ILOVESQL' --Here password is in uppercase

SELECT      * FROM      dbo.Users WHERE    userName = 'James' AND
password = 'ilovesql'--Here password is in lowercase

SELECT      * FROM      dbo.Users WHERE    userName = 'James' AND
password = 'IloveSQL'--Here password is in exact case
```

Output:

	id	userName	password
1	1	James	IloveSQL

	id	userName	password
1	1	James	IloveSQL

	id	userName	password
1	1	James	IloveSQL

Here all the three queries return the result because SQL Server does not perform case sensitive search.

Example B:

```
SELECT * FROM dbo.Users WHERE userName = 'James' AND
CAST(password AS varbinary(15)) = CAST('ILOVESQL' AS
varbinary(15))  --Here password is in uppercase

SELECT * FROM dbo.Users WHERE userName = 'James' AND
CAST(password AS varbinary(15)) = CAST('ilovesql' AS
varbinary(15)) --Here password is in lowercase

SELECT       * FROM       dbo.Users WHERE   userName = 'James' AND
CAST(password AS varbinary(15)) = CAST('IloveSQL' AS
varbinary(15)) --Here password is in exact case
```

Here *password* column is casted to VARBINARY type and then compared, so the search is case-sensitive.

Output:

11.   How to select wildcard characters _ or % using LIKE?

We can able to do this in two ways,

➤ Enclose the wildcards by bracket
  o To search "100% free" use "100[%] free"
  o To search "[" use "[[]"
➤ Using ESCAPE clause
  o To search "_" (underscore) use '@_' ESCAPE '@'
  o Or to search "_"(underscore) use 'A_' ESCAPE 'A'
  ESCAPE character may be anything

Syntax:

```
LIKE '[<<Wild Character to search>>]'



LIKE '<<Escape character>><<Wild Character to search>>' ESCAPE
'<<Escape character>>'
```

Example:

```
USE Demo
GO

SELECT * FROM Tbl_Sample WHERE [name] LIKE '100[%]%'
GO

SELECT * FROM Tbl_Sample WHERE [name] LIKE '[[]]C%'
GO

SELECT * FROM Tbl_Sample WHERE [name] LIKE '@_%' ESCAPE '@'
-- OR

SELECT * FROM Tbl_Sample WHERE [name] LIKE 'A_%' ESCAPE 'A'
```

Output:

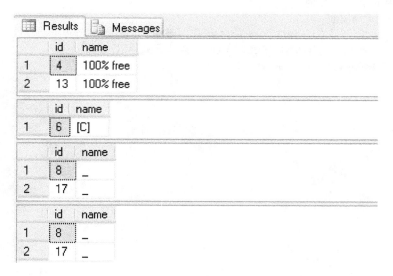

12.   How to pause and execute the query?

We can do this using WAITFOR DELAY statement. When SQL Server encounters the WAITFOR DELAY statement it will pause the execution process for the specified period.

Syntax:

```
WAITFOR DELAY 'hh:mm:ss' --Hours : Minutes : Seconds
```

Example:

```
SELECT getdate()

GO

WAITFOR DELAY '0:0:15'

GO



SELECT getdate() -It will execute after 15 seconds
```

Output:

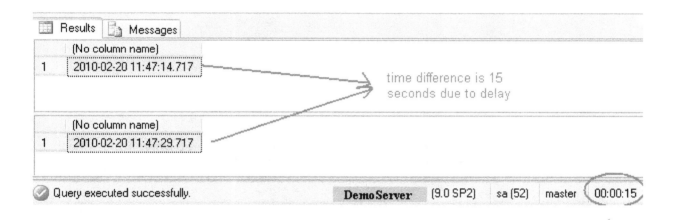

In the above example second getdate() function get executed after 15 seconds delay.

13.   How to solve server time out problem?

Most of the people complaint about "server time out" problem. The common causes and solutions are explained here.

Causes

 ➢ Due to long running query
 ➢ Due to dead lock/locks.

Solutions

➢ If we are getting "server time out" in that particular query or SP and it is really a time consuming one, then we have to increase the command/query time out for that particular query or SP.
➢ If the problem is due to dead lock/locks then the following solution will help you to avoid this situation.

Scenario simulation

Step #1 Open SQL Server Management Studio
Step #2 Open a new query window and execute the following query.

```
USE Demo

BEGIN TRAN

UPDATE dbo.Country SET code = 'USA' WHERE code ='US'
```

Don't commit or rollback the transaction now

Step #3 Open another query window and execute the following query.

```
SELECT * FROM dbo.Country
```

Now the query execution can not complete and keep on waiting. Because the transaction **Step #2** holds the lock on the table.

Output

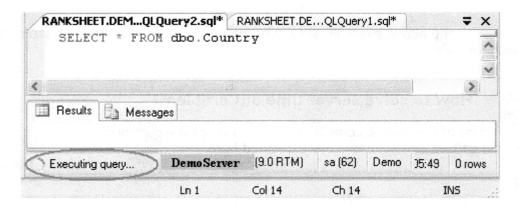

Step #4 Open another new Query window and execute the following query.

```
SELECT * FROM dbo.Country WITH (NOLOCK)
```

Now the query executes immediately and returns the result of 4 records including the locked record *USA*. The NOLOCK hint does not consider about locks it can even fetch records which the table is locked. i.e. NOLOCK performs dirty reads.

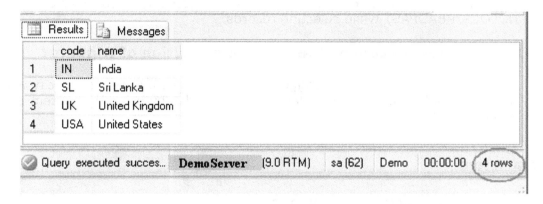

Step #5 Open another new Query window and execute the following query.

```
SELECT * FROM dbo.Country WITH (READPAST)
```

Now the query executes immediately and returns 3 records other than the record *USA*. The READPAST hint does not include locked records. But the problem is that the total records selected may vary based on locks.

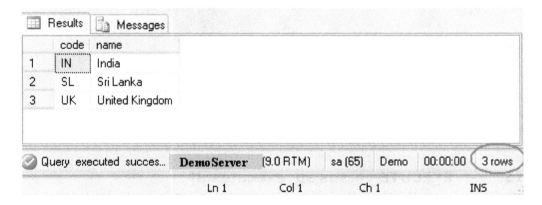

Step #6 Now check **Step #3** window, it still showing as executing.
Step #7 Go to **Step #1** window and type the following code, execute the code alone by highlighting.

```
ROLLBACK TRAN
```

Step #8 Check **Step #3** window, the query execution is now completed.

Note:

In real-world database applications, approximately 80% database operations are data read operations and only 20% are data write operations. For INSERT/UPDATE/DELETE operation locks are necessary, so consider using NOLOCK/READPAST while selecting records.

14. How to control the order of execution of triggers?

We cannot decide the trigger execution order, but we can specify which trigger should execute first and last. We can do this by using the system-stored procedure sp_settriggerorder.

Parameters

1. **name** – name of the trigger
2. **order** - FIRST/ LAST/NONE
3. **type** - INSERT/UPDATE/DELETE

If the *order* value is NONE then the execution order is automatic.

Syntax:

```
EXEC sp_settriggerorder '<<Trigger name>>', 'FIRST/LAST/NONE',
'INSERT/UPDATE/DELETE'
```

Example:

```
--Specify the Tr_ Identity_Test as first trigger to execute

EXEC sp_settriggerorder 'Tr_ Identity_Test', 'FIRST', 'INSERT'
```

15. EXECUTE versus sp_executesql?

EXECUTE command is also shortly known as EXEC, which is used to execute stored procedure and dynamic queries.

sp_executesql is a system-stored procedure especially used to execute dynamic queries. The advantage of using *sp_executesql* is, it also support parameterized queries.

While executing dynamic queries with parameter *sp_executesql*, it will reuse the execution plan and improve the performance

EXECUTE:

While passing dynamic queries to EXECUTE command, parenthesis is must.

Syntax:

```
EXECUTE ('<<Dynamic sql>>')

-- OR

EXEC ('<<Dynamic sql>>')
```

Example A:

```
EXECUTE ('SELECT * FROM Country')

-- OR

EXEC ('SELECT * FROM Country')
```

sp_executesql:

sp_executesql only accepts NVARCHAR type. If we want to directly pass VARCHAR as argument, we need to explicitly convert VARCHAR to NVARCHAR.
Adding character 'N' as prefix will cast VARCHAR to NVARCHAR ('N' prefix should be in upper case)

Syntax:

```
EXEC SP_EXECUTESQL '<<string in nvarchar format>>'

EXEC SP_EXECUTESQL N'<<string>>'
```

Example B:

```
EXEC SP_EXECUTESQL N'SELECT  *  FROM Country'
```

16.   How to find space consumption of database or table?

To find how much space a table or a database is consuming, use *sp_spaceused* system stored procedure.

To find the database space consumption

Syntax:

```
USE <<Database>>

EXEC sp_spaceused
```

Example A:

```
USE Demo

EXEC sp_spaceused
```

Output:

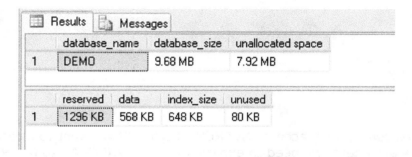

To find the table space consumption

Syntax B:

```
USE <<Database>>
EXEC sp_spaceused '<<Table name>>'
```

Example:

```
USE Demo
EXEC sp_spaceused 'dbo.Tbl_Sample'
```

Output:

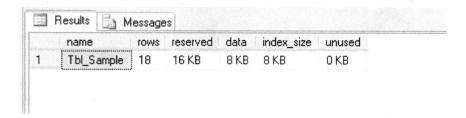

17.   What is the fastest way to find number of rows in a table?

There are two ways to find the number of rows in a table.

Usual Way:

Using COUNT(*) function, we can get the number of rows in a table.

Example A:

```
USE Demo
SELECT COUNT(*) FROM dbo.BigTable
```

Output:

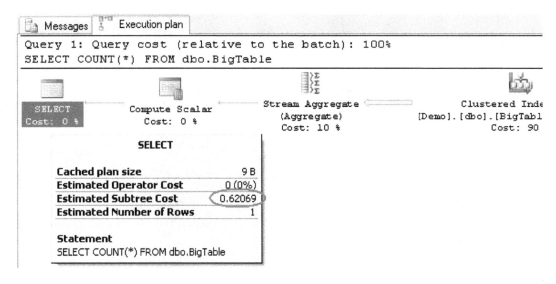

Here estimated sub tree cost is 0.62069

This is the common way but not the fastest way. This query statement requires a full table scan or full clustered index scan to find the total number of rows.

Fastest Way:

Using *sysindexes* system-table, we can find the number of rows in a table without any scans.

Syntax:

```
SELECT rows FROM sysindexes

WHERE id = OBJECT_ID ('<<Table Name>>')AND indid < 2
```

Example B:

```
USE Demo

SELECT rows FROM sysindexes

WHERE id = OBJECT_ID ('dbo.BigTable')AND indid < 2
```

Output:

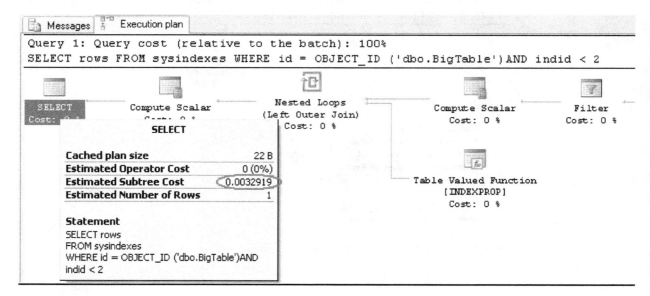

Here estimated sub tree cost is 0.0032919

The *rows* column in the *sysindexes* system-table keeps the current row count information. If table has a clustered index then *indid* is 1 else *indid* is 0. Always use the condition *indid* < 2 condition in WHERE clause.

Conclusion:

As per the test, example B executes 180 times faster than example A.

Note:

BigTable does not contain any records to populate records, use the following script. Script is in the file Solution_17Data.sql

Script to populate *BigTable*:

```
USE Demo

GO

-- Query batch to insert 100000 records

DECLARE @I INT

SET @I = 1

WHILE @I <= 100000

    BEGIN

        INSERT INTO dbo.BigTable (guid, id, description)
VALUES( NEWID(),@I , 'TEST DATA #' +CONVERT(VARCHAR,@I) );

        SET @I =@I + 1

    END
```

18. How to use TOP *n* PERCENT, TOP *n* and TOP WITH TIES clause?

TOP <n> PERCENT

The TOP *n* PERCENT indicates that the query returns only the first *n* percentage of rows from the base result set. For example TOP 50 PERCENT query returns only 6 records of 12 records, which means 50% of the rows.

Syntax:

```
SELECT TOP <N> PERCENT  <column_name>/* FROM <TableName>
```

Example:

```
SELECT * FROM Employee_Salary
```

Output:

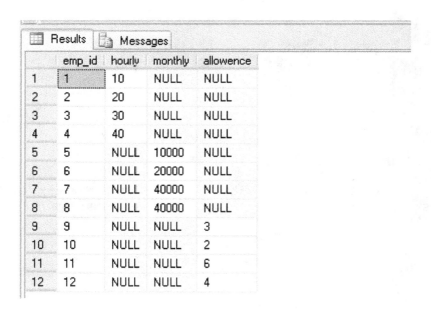

Selecting *Employee_Salary* table without TOP clause returns 12 records.

Example:

```
SELECT TOP 50 PERCENT * FROM Employee_Salary
```

Output:

	emp_id	hourlye	monthly	allowence
1	1	10	NULL	NULL
2	2	20	NULL	NULL
3	3	30	NULL	NULL
4	4	40	NULL	NULL
5	5	NULL	10000	NULL
6	6	NULL	20000	NULL

TOP <n>

SELECT TOP N statement will returns exactly N records from the base result set.

Syntax:

```
SELECT TOP <N> <column_name>/* FROM <TableName>
```

Example:

```
SELECT TOP 6 PERCENT * FROM Employee_Salary
```

TOP WITH TIES

If TOP WITH TIES specified in the query, additional rows with the same values will be returned from the base result in the ORDER BY columns appearing as the last of the TOP n (PERCENT) rows. TOP WITH TIES can only be used with ORDER BY clause.

Syntax:

```
SELECT TOP N PERCENT WITH TIES  column1,column2  FROM TableName
ORDER BY column1 DESC
```

Example(With Out WITH TIES):

```
SELECT TOP 3 id,monthly FROM Employee_Salary WHERE monthly IS NOT
NULL ORDER BY monthly
```

Output:

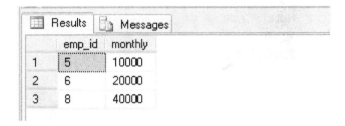

Here the query returns exactly 3 records.

Example(With WITH TIES):

```
SELECT TOP 3 WITH TIES id,monthly FROM Employee_Salary WHERE
monthly IS NOT NULL ORDER BY monthly
```

Output:

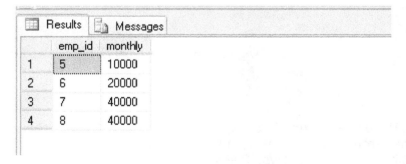

Now the query returns 4 records while using WITH TIES.

19.   How to get the remote computer name from SQL Server?

We can get the remote computer name using system function HOST_NAME.

Example:

```
SELECT HOST_NAME()
```

Where to Use:

This feature can be used in some client-server application for security. The application can identify from which machine the request is coming to the server.

Note:

If we use the *HOST_NAME* in web application such as ASP, then it only returns the web server name and not the client machine name.

20.   Why should not use BINARY_CHECKSUM() for case sensitive searches?

BINARY_CHECKSUM function is commonly used to compare strings. This technique only works fine with shorter strings.

Example A:

```
SELECT

BINARY_CHECKSUM('ABCD') AS [Checksum value for 'ABCD'],
BINARY_CHECKSUM('abcd') AS [Checksum value for 'abcd']
```

Output:

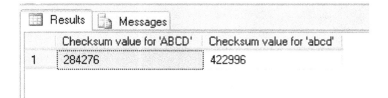

	Checksum value for 'ABCD'	Checksum value for 'abcd'
1	284276	422996

BINARY_CHECKSUM() is not suitable for comparing longer strings. The following query will crack BINARY_CHECKSUM function and returns the same checksum value for two different inputs.

Example B:

```
SELECT

BINARY_CHECKSUM('A') AS [Checksum value for 'A'],
BINARY_CHECKSUM('AAAAAAAAAAAAAAAA') AS [Checksum value for
'AAAAAAAAAAAAAAAA']
```

Output:

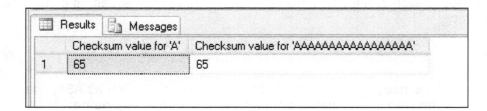

So we recommend using binary conversion method for case sensitive searches. *[Reference: Solution 10]*

21.   How to use INSERT <<Table Name>> DEFAULT VALUES?

This statement will insert default values to the given table without prompting any input. But all the *not null* columns in the table should contain default values.

Syntax:

```
INSERT <<Table Name>> DEFAULT VALUES
```

Example:

```
INSERT [Log] DEFAULT VALUES
```

Structure of *Log* Table

	Name	Owner	Type	Created_datetime
1	Log	dbo	user table	2010-03-23 10:25:32.577

	Column_name	Type	Com...	Length	Prec	Scale	Nul...	TrimTraili...	Fixed...	Collation
1	id	numeric	no	9	18	0	no	(n/a)	(n/a)	NULL
2	Description	varchar	no	50			no	no	no	SQL_Lati...
3	CreatedAt	datetime	no	8			no	(n/a)	(n/a)	NULL
4	CreatedBy	varchar	no	50			no	no	no	SQL_Lati...

	Identity	Seed	Increment	Not For Replication
1	id	1	1	0

	RowGuidCol
1	No rowguidcol column defined.

	Data_located_on_filegroup
1	PRIMARY

Default values for NOTNULL columns

	index_name	index_description	index_keys
1	PK_Tbl_Log	clustered, unique, primary key located on PRIMARY	id

	constraint_type	constraint_...	delet...	upd...	statu...	status_for_r...	constraint_keys
1	DEFAULT on column CreatedAt	DF__Log_...	(n/a)	(n/a)	(n/a)	(n/a)	(getdate())
2	DEFAULT on column CreatedBy	DF__Log_...	(n/a)	(n/a)	(n/a)	(n/a)	(suser_sname())
3	DEFAULT on column Descripti...	DF__Log_...	(n/a)	(n/a)	(n/a)	(n/a)	('')
4	PRIMARY KEY (clustered)	PK_Tbl_Log	(n/a)	(n/a)	(n/a)	(n/a)	id

Note:

In the above example all the *not null* column of table *Log* have default values and primary key is identity column. So the above statement will execute any number of times without prompting. For every execution, it will create new record with default values.

22.   How to get the latest identity value of the table in different ways?

The following example returns results after execute an INSERT statement only.

@@IDENTITY

@@IDENTITY is a system global variable. We can get the last generated identity value with in the session (session can contain multiple scopes).

Syntax:

```
SELECT @@IDENTITY
```

IDENT_CURRENT

Using IDENT_CURRENT function, we can get the last generated identity value of a specific table name within the session.

Syntax:

```
SELECT IDENT_CURRENT ('<<Table Name>>')
```

SCOPE_IDENTITY

Using SCOPE_IDENTITY function, we can get the last generated identity field value within the scope.

Syntax:

```
SELECT SCOPE_IDENTITY()
```

@@IDENTITY versus SCOPE_IDENTITY

People commonly use @@identity to get the latest generated identity value after the insert statement. Beware!, if the insert statement triggers some other insert statement then the @@IDENTITY variable returns the identity value of the trigger generated insert statement not the statement executed inside the scope. So we recommend using SCOPE_IDENTITY in this kind of situation.

Example A:

```
INSERT INTO Identity_test values ('ONE')

SELECT @@IDENTITY AS '@@IDENTITY'

SELECT IDENT_CURRENT ('Identity_test') AS IDENT_CURRENT

SELECT SCOPE_IDENTITY() AS SCOPE_IDENTITY
```

Output:

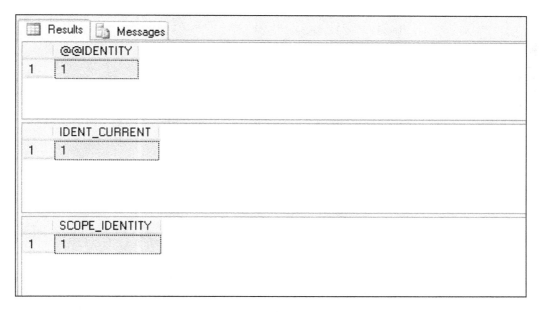

For the table *Identity_test*, all the functions return the expected result.

Example 2:

```
INSERT INTO Identity_test2 values ('ONE')

SELECT @@IDENTITY AS '@@IDENTITY'

SELECT IDENT_CURRENT ('Identity_test2') AS IDENT_CURRENT

SELECT SCOPE_IDENTITY() AS SCOPE_IDENTITY
```

Output:

	@@IDENTITY
1	10

	IDENT_CURRENT
1	1

	SCOPE_IDENTITY
1	1

In the above case @@IDENTITY fails to return correct value, because table *Identity_Test2 is* having a trigger *Tr_Identity_Test,* which inserts a record to the table *Identity_Op.* so @@IDENTITY returns the identity value of table *Identity_Op* not *Identity_Test .*Because @@IDENTITY always returns the last identity value generated within the session.

23.   What is the recommended order to create index?

First create the clustered index before creating any non-clustered index in the table. Clustered index control the order of records stored in the database. The non-clustered indexes relay on clustered index.

For example, if we create non-clustered index for a table which does not have clustered index, SQL Server creates an integer column for the internal use and identify rows based on the column. Later if we create clustered index followed by non-clustered indexes for the same table then we have to use *dbcc dbreindex* command to rebuild the indexes. It rebuilds all index of the table.

Syntax:

```
dbcc dbreindex ('<Table name>')
```

NOTE:

Always create clustered index first, so that we can avoid rebuilding the indexes.

24.   What is the difference between unique and unique index?

  Unique is a constraint definition enforce validation, it automatically creates index to speed up performance. *Unique* does not allow duplicate values. *Index* is a storage structure, only used for performance. In *index* duplicates can be allowed, but in *unique index* duplicates are not allowed.

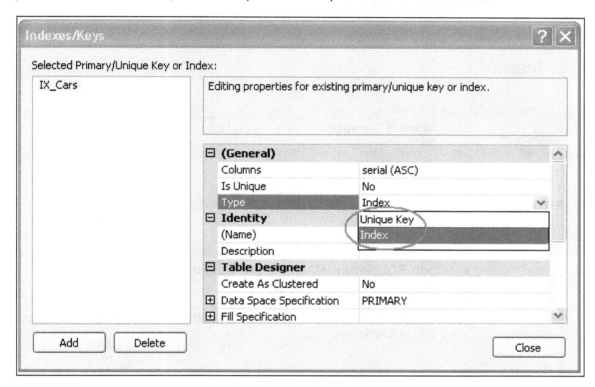

25.   How to make entire database as read only?

  Using *sp_dboption* system stored procedure we can make the database as read only.

<u>Syntax:</u>

```
EXEC Sp_DbOption '<<Database name>>','read only','<<TRUE/FALSE>>'
```

Example:

```
EXEC Sp_DbOption 'Demo','read only','TRUE'

-- Run the following command to change back to default state

EXEC Sp_DbOption 'Demo','read only','FALSE'
```

Output:

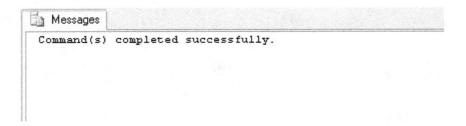

Using GUI

> Open SQL Server Management Studio
> Open properties of the database
> Go to Options page
> Change the Database Read-Only property under State category to true and click OK

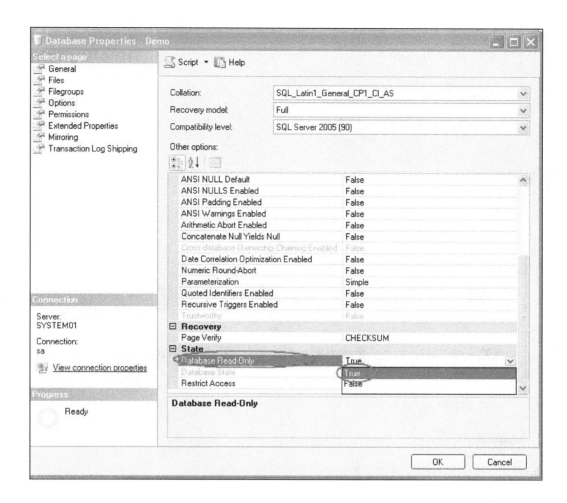

Where to use:

Read-only databases are necessary for statistics reports and also to prevent database from accidental changes.

26.   How to enter null values explicitly from SQL Server Management Studio?

We can do this in any one of the following methods
- Just hold down control key and press 0, to enter null value explicitly (**Ctrl+0**)
- Type *null* in lower case and move to next cell
- Copy and paste the *null* value from some other cell.

ationKey	designationId	designationOther	dob
3OPM	2		NULL
PCK0	2		NULL
QMK8	NULL	NULL	NULL
PRP7W	NULL	NULL	NULL
3GTZ4	NULL	NULL	NULL
TS5V	NULL	NULL	NULL
FWPH	2		NULL
EA879	NULL	NULL	NULL
7IZ6	NULL	NULL	NULL

Note:

This is not a new feature in SQL Server 2005, this feature is already available since SQL Server 2000. We need to install latest service pack to use **Ctrl+0** in SQL Server 2005.

27.   How to get date time instead of using Getdate()?

We can use CURRENT_TIMESTAMP to get the date time value without database time zone offset.

Example:

```
SELECT CURRENT_TIMESTAMP
```

28.   How to rename the database and table?

We can do that using system stored procedure or from GUI. We can use sp_rename to rename both database and table.

To rename Database

We can use the specialized system stored procedure *sp_renamedb* to rename database.

Syntax:

```
sp_renamedb '<<db name>>','<<new db name>>'

-- Or

sp_rename  '<<db name>>','<<new db name>>', 'DATABASE'
```

Example:

```
sp_renamedb 'old_name','new_name'

-- OR

sp_rename 'old_name','new_name', 'DATABASE'
```

To rename Table

Syntax:

```
sp_rename '<<table name>>','<<new table name>>'
```

Example:

```
sp_rename 'old_table_name','new_table_name'
```

GUI:

From SQL Server Management Studio, right click on the database/table and click rename to change the name.

NOTE:

By using *sp_rename* we cannot rename stored procedures, view, UDF and trigger.

29.   How to use UNION and UNION ALL?

Both are used to combine the result-set of two or more queries into a single result set. UNION also does distinct. UNION ALL does not check for duplicate records, so it is faster than UNION during combining results.

If we want to combine result-sets and definitely know the result set does not contain any duplicate records then use UNION ALL instead of UNION to improve performance.

Syntax:

```
<<Query1>> UNION ALL <<Query2>>
```

Example:

```
SELECT code,name FROM Country

UNION ALL

SELECT CONVERT(CHAR(10),ID),name FROM Tbl_Sample
```

30.   How to disable auto commit mode?

By default SQL Server works under auto commit mode. When we execute any insert/delete/update statements, SQL Server automatically commits the changes if there is no error. If we disable the auto commit mode we need to explicitly commit or rollback.

To disable auto commit mode use SET IMPLICIT_TRANSACTIONS ON

Syntax:

```
SET IMPLICIT_TRANSACTIONS <<ON / OFF>>
```

To enable auto commit mode use SET IMPLICIT_TRANSACTIONS OFF

Example:

```
SET IMPLICIT_TRANSACTIONS ON

DELETE FROM Identity_test

SELECT * FROM Identity_test

ROLLBACK

SELECT * FROM Identity_test

SET IMPLICIT_TRANSACTIONS OFF
```

Output:

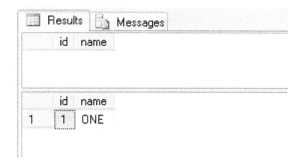

Caution:

By default IMPLICIT_TRANSACTIONS property is off. So the statements are committed immediately. When we work with implicit transaction ON, other connections cannot use the affected tables until you explicitly commit or rollback.

31.　　How to improve the data import performance in a table which is having constraint?

Data import performance will be degraded due to validation checks during large import process, if the table has constraints. Disable the constraints before importing the large data to the table. This will speed up the importing process. Enable the constraints after importing data.

Syntax:

```
-- Disable Constraint

ALTER TABLE <<Table_name>> NOCHECK CONSTRAINT <<constraint_name>>

-- Enable Constraint

ALTER TABLE <<Table_name>> CHECK CONSTRAINT <<constraint_name>>
```

32.　　How to improve the performance of replication?

Disabling and enabling the constraint is not an ideal solution for replication, because replication process is a daily activity. Add the NOT FOR REPLICATION option, while defining constraints in the table. This option forces SQL Server not to validate records during the replication process.

Syntax:

```
CONSTRAINT <<Constraint name>> CHECK NOT FOR REPLICATION
(<<Constraint condition comes here>>)
```

33.   How to improve the performance of stored procedure?

➢ Use SET NOCOUNT ON to avoid sending row count information for every statement.
➢ Always use the owner name or schema name before the object name to prevent recompilation of stored procedures.
➢ Avoid using DISTINCT.
➢ Minimize the number of columns in SELECT clause.
➢ Use table variables instead of temporary tables.
➢ Use the CTE (Common Table expression) instead of derived tables and table variables as much as possible.
➢ Avoid using cursors.
➢ Don't use duplicate codes, reuse the code by using Views and UDFs.
➢ Begin and commit transactions immediately.
➢ Avoid exclusive locks.
➢ Use table hints.

34.   SELECT versus RETURN?

SELECT can return single value or record-set but RETURN statement can only returns single value.

In case of returning a single value, choose RETURN for better performance. Because SQL Server does not create record-set object while using RETURN statement and it does not execute any statements followed by RETURN statement.

35.   How to get current database user name?

SYSTEM_USER function returns the current database user name. Authentication may be either windows authentication or SQL Server authentication.

Example:

```
SELECT SYSTEM_USER
```

36.   How to use CURRENT_USER?

CURRENT_USER returns different possible results based on database user role.

➤ If database user is member of *sysadmin* server role, then returns "dbo".
➤ If database user is not a member of *sysadmin* server role and has access to the current database, then returns database user name.
➤ If database user is not a member of *sysadmin* server role and does not have access to the current database then returns "guest".

Example:

```
SELECT CURRENT_USER
```

37.   CROSS JOIN versus INNER JOIN?

CROSS JOIN is similar to INNER JOIN, but does not have ON clause. So, while using CROSS JOIN have to use WHERE clause instead of ON clause.
CROSS JOINs are normally used to produce test data, and been occasionally used.

Example:

```
USE DEMO

-- Using INNER JOIN

SELECT E.* , S.* FROM Employee as E INNER JOIN Employee_Salary S
ON

E.employeeid = S.id

WHERE title = 'Inside Sales Coordinator'

-- Using CROSS JOIN

SELECT E.* , S.* FROM Employee as E CROSS JOIN Employee_Salary S
WHERE E.employeeid = S.id

AND title = 'Inside Sales Coordinator'
```

Output:

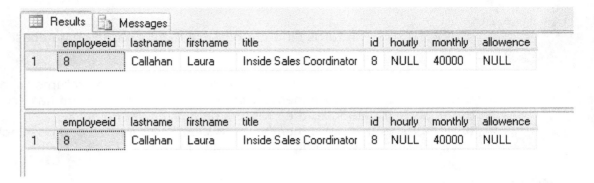

	employeeid	lastname	firstname	title	id	hourly	monthly	allowence
1	8	Callahan	Laura	Inside Sales Coordinator	8	NULL	40000	NULL

	employeeid	lastname	firstname	title	id	hourly	monthly	allowence
1	8	Callahan	Laura	Inside Sales Coordinator	8	NULL	40000	NULL

Here both queries return the same result.

38.   How to improve the performance of JOINs?

- ➢ JOIN operation performance can be improved by indexing the columns involved in the JOIN clause.
- ➢ WHERE clause will execute before the JOIN clause. So restricting the number of records using WHERE clause will reduce the rows involved in the JOIN process.
- ➢ Always access the column names with alias name or table name in the query. If SQL Server encounters column name without any prefixes, it have to search the column name in the contributed table's column collection.
- ➢ Choose when to use WHERE clause or HAVING clause. WHERE clause evaluates before the GROUP BY clause. HAVING clause evaluates after generating the group columns and aggregative functions such as COUNT, MIN, MAX, etc,… can only be used in HAVING clause not in WHERE clause.

39.   How to improve the performance of CURSOR?

- ➢ Restrict unwanted rows by minimizing the conditions inside the cursor loop and maximize the conditions while opening cursor.
- ➢ If the cursor is read-only and deals with large number of tables, better insert the record set into a temporary table and open the temporary table using cursor.
- ➢ By default all cursors are global. Global cursors can be used anywhere in the same session. Local cursors are valid only within the scope. Choose the appropriate cursor based on the requirement.
- ➢ Choose the appropriate cursor behavior, recommended behavior is FAST_FORWARD

➢ Choose the appropriate cursor type. We can combine FORWARD_ONLY with any cursor types.
➢ Avoid locks, try to use READ_ONLY lock.
➢ After closing the cursor, the structure will not be destroyed immediately, only the locks will be released. But we cannot retrieve rows after closing the cursor.
➢ To use optimal memory, deallocate the cursor. After deallocating the cursor we cannot open the cursor again.
➢ Cursors definitely slow down the performance. Try to avoid cursors by using sub quires, UDFs and CTE.

40.   How to handle transactions better?

➢ While using nested transaction, it does not commit immediately even we commit the inner transaction. It waits for external transaction to commit. The *@@trancount* system variable should be 0 when committing.
➢ Nested transactions are not advisable.
➢ If we pass transaction name as argument while using COMMIT TRANSACTION *<name>*, the name will be ignored and the last transaction will only be committed.
➢ Even we rollback the internal transaction, the SQL Server rollbacks all the transactions.
➢ Transaction names are case sensitive
➢ In ROLLBACK TRANSACTION statement the only allowed name is, outer most transaction name or save point name. If we use the inner transaction name the SQL Server throws error.
➢ In complicated transaction, it is advised to use WITH MARK option. Because we can able to restore database to previous state in case of any accidents.

Syntax:

```
BEGIN TRAN <Transaction name> WITH MARK
```

41.   How to do validation using views?

Structure of *Labor* table

	Column_name	Type	Computed	Length	F :	Nullable	TrimTrailingBlanks	FixedLenN
1	EmpNo	char	no	5		no	no	no
2	Name	varchar	no	30		no	no	no
3	Description	varchar	no	100		yes	no	yes

If we want to apply a business rule in *Labor* table as follows.

> ➤ *EmpNo* column value should only accept values starting with 'E'.
> ➤ *EmpNo* column length should not be less than 5.
> ➤ *Description* column value should not be null (Already it is a *Nullable* column)

We can use CHECK constraint and make the description column as NOT NULL column. But the existing data can contain null values. In future the business rule may get changed. For this situation, the better method is to use WITH CHECK OPTION in VIEW.

Write the following query to satisfy the business requirement.

Example A

```
SELECT

        EmpNo ,

        Name ,

        Description

FROM

        Labor

WHERE

EmpNo LIKE 'E%'              AND

LEN(EmpNo) = 5              AND

DESCRIPTION IS NOT NULL AND

DESCRIPTION <> ''
```

Create the query as VIEW by adding "WITH CHECK OPTION" in the end of query. Now the view is ready to validate the business rule. If we try to insert values which do not satisfy the business rule, we will get an error.

Syntax:

```
CREATE VIEW <<View name>>

AS

<<Select Statement with the required filter>> WITH CHECK OPTION

GO
```

Example B(Create view using WITH CHECK OPTION):

```sql
CREATE VIEW Vew_Labor_Rule1
AS
SELECT
        EmpNo,
        Name,
        Description
FROM
        Labor
WHERE
        EmpNo LIKE 'E%'             AND
        LEN(EmpNo) = 5             AND
        DESCRIPTION IS NOT NULL AND
        DESCRIPTION <> '' WITH CHECK OPTION


GO
```

<u>Example C (Attempt to insert invalid records using view):</u>

```
-- This insert statement throw error due to EmplNo lenght is not
equal to 5

INSERT INTO Vew_Labor_Rule1 (EmpNo,Name,Description)
VALUES('E02','Dame','System Engineer')


-- This insert statement throw error due to EmplNo not start with
E

INSERT INTO Vew_Labor_Rule1 (EmpNo,Name,Description)
VALUES('0002','James','Developer')


-- This insert statement throw error due to Description string is
empty

INSERT INTO Vew_Labor_Rule1 (EmpNo,Name,Description)
VALUES('E0002','Jhon','')


-- This insert statement throw error due to Description value is
null

INSERT INTO Vew_Labor_Rule1 (EmpNo,Name,Description)
VALUES('E0002','David',null)


-- This insert statement throw error due to Description value is
not specified

INSERT INTO Vew_Labor_Rule1 (EmpNo,Name) VALUES('E0002','Wes')
```

```
Messages
Msg 550, Level 16, State 1, Line 2
The attempted insert or update failed because the target view either
 specifies WITH CHECK OPTION or spans a view that specifies
 WITH CHECK OPTION and one or more rows resulting from the
operation did not qualify under the CHECK OPTION constraint.
The statement has been terminated.
Msg 550, Level 16, State 1, Line 5
The attempted insert or update failed because the target view either spe
The statement has been terminated.
Msg 550, Level 16, State 1, Line 8
The attempted insert or update failed because the target view either spe
The statement has been terminated.
Msg 550, Level 16, State 1, Line 11
The attempted insert or update failed because the target view either spe
The statement has been terminated.
```

Example D (Insert valid records using view):

```
-- following insert statements will successfully insert

INSERT INTO Vew_Labor_Rule1 (EmpNo, Name, Description)
VALUES('E0002','Dame','System Engineer')


INSERT INTO Vew_Labor_Rule1 (EmpNo, Name, Description)
VALUES('E0003','Gina','Telecom Engineer')
```

Output:

```
Messages

(1 row(s) affected)

(1 row(s) affected)
```

Note:

For this type of uncertain business rules, above solution will help.

42.   Known and Unknown things about trigger?

➢ Two types of DML triggers are there, AFTER and INSTEAD OF triggers.
➢ Views can have only INSTEAD OF trigger.
➢ We cannot create INSTEAD OF trigger for a view, which is created using WITH CHECK OPTION.
➢ FOR is equivalent to AFTER keyword. FOR keyword is still valid for compatibility.
➢ We can use the UPDATE() function in the trigger to find whether a particular column is changed. It returns bit value 1 if the column is changed.
➢ We can use the function COLUMNS_UPDATED()in the trigger to find whether a set of columns are changed in single statement. It returns sequence of bits with the update status of every column.
➢ We cannot change the name of a trigger using the *sp_rename*, to rename a trigger it is recommended to drop and recreate the trigger again.
➢ We can enable and disable triggers.
➢ SQL Server 2005 supports DDL triggers

Syntax:

```
--Disable Trigger

 ALTER TABLE <<Table_name>> DISABLE TRIGGER <trigger_name(s)>   |
ALL

--Enable Trigger

ALTER TABLE <<Table_name>> ENABLE TRIGGER <trigger_name(s)>   |
ALL
```

Example:

```
--Disable Trigger

 ALTER TABLE Identity_Test2 DISABLE TRIGGER ALL

--Enable Trigger

 ALTER TABLE Identity_Test2 ENABLE TRIGGER ALL
```

43. How to use BULK INSERT?

BULK INSERT statement is used to import data from file into a table or view.

Following example explains how to import data from a .csv file to a table. A sample data is stored in "C:\Script\Solutions\bulkdata.txt" (SQL Server locates the file in host machine not in the client machine)

Bulkdata.txt

```
E0008,Brown,System Engineer
E0009,Jordan,Software Engineer
E0010,Ritz,Database Developer
E0011,Joseph,Database Admin
```

Example:

```sql
USE Demo

BULK INSERT Labor

FROM 'C:\Script\solutions\bulkdata.txt'

WITH

(

FIELDTERMINATOR =',',

ROWTERMINATOR ='\n'

)

SELECT * FROM Labor
```

Output:

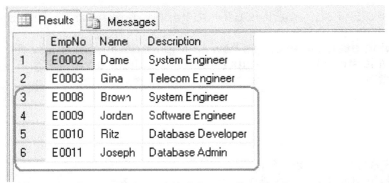

Now 4 records newly added from the file into the *Labor* table.

NOTE

> ➢ Path of the .csv file should be in FROM clause.
> ➢ FIELDTERMINATOR and ROWTERMINATOR seperator value depends on the file, in this case of .csv file
>   > o FIELDTERMINATOR is (,)
>   > o ROWTERMINATOR is (\n).

44.   How to test the performance of a particular query constantly?

We can test the performance of a query using the DBCC DROPCLEANBUFFERS command.

This command removes the entire buffer from memory and force the query not to use any buffers.

Syntax:

```
DBCC DROPCLEANBUFFERS
```

45. Compiling SQL statements?

When NOEXE flag is turned on, SQL Server does not execute any queries and it only checks the query for syntax error. Even SQL Server does not throw any errors when the query containing database object names which does not exist.

Syntax:

```
SET NOEXEC ON.
```

To use this feature from GUI, click "Parse" button in toolbar (Cntrl+F5)

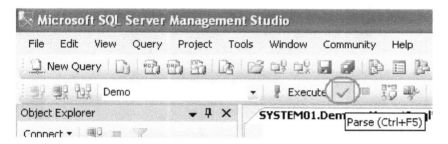

46. How to use COALESCE function?

COALESCE returns the first non-null value among its arguments.

Syntax:

```
COALESCE (expression1, expression2, ... expression N )
```

Example A:

```
SELECT COALESCE (NULL,NULL,20,100,NULL)
```

For the above example, COALESCE returns the value 20. Because "20" is the first non-null value.

Output:

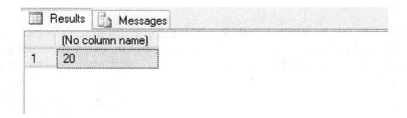

Example B:

Employee_Salary table contains three columns *hourly, monthly, allowence.* The following query returns the non-null value among the three columns.

```
USE Demo

SELECT emp_id,COALESCE (hourly,monthly,allowence) as 'salary'
FROM Employee_Salary
```

Output:

	emp_id	salary
1	1	10
2	2	20
3	3	30
4	4	40
5	5	10000
6	6	20000
7	7	40000
8	8	40000
9	9	3
10	10	2
11	11	6
12	12	4

47.   Known and unknown things about TIMESTAMP datatype?

> The TIMESTAMP is a special kind of datatype. The value of the TIMESTAMP column automatically updated when the row changed.
> The TIMESTAMP columns does not contain date time information
> A table can have only one TIMESTAMP column.
> The TIMESTAMP datatype has no relation to the system time and it is simply a monotonically increasing counter whose values will always be unique within a database.
> While inserting record into a table containing TIMESTAMP column, TIMESTAMP column automatically gets value.
> We cannot insert values explicitly to TIMESTAMP column.
> We can able to set default value for TIMESTAMP column.
> For replication process, TIMESTAMP columns are recommended.
> The synonym for the TIMESTAMP datatype is ROWVERSION

Example:

```
USE Demo

SELECT *  FROM [Timestamp_Demo]

UPDATE Timestamp_Demo SET [name] = 'new value updated' WHERE id = 1

SELECT *  FROM [Timestamp_Demo]
```

Output:

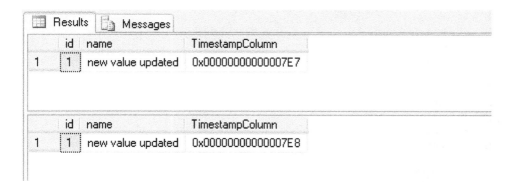

We can able to execute the above example query any numbers of times, after updating any column in the *Timestamp_Demo* table. *TimestampColumn* column value automatically gets changed.

48.   How to use SOME and ALL operators?

SOME and ALL are used to compare scalar value with single-column result set. Both can be used in SQL or PL/SQL.

SOME:

SOME and ANY are equivalent. The following query returns TRUE because 15 is less than some of the values in the table *Employee_Salary*.

Example:

```
SELECT id,hourly FROM Employee_Salary

GO

IF 15 < SOME (SELECT hourly FROM dbo.Employee_Salary)

SELECT 'TRUE'

ELSE

SELECT 'FALSE' ;
```

Output:

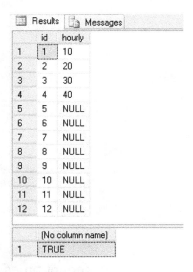

ALL:

The following query returns FALSE because 15 is not less than all of the values in the table *Employee_Salary*.

Example:

```
SELECT id,hourly FROM Employee_Salary

GO

IF 15 < ALL (SELECT hourly FROM dbo.Employee_Salary)

SELECT 'TRUE'

ELSE

SELECT 'FALSE' ;
```

Output:

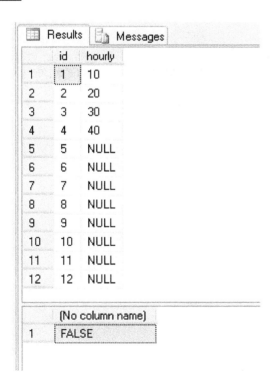

49.   REPLACE versus STUFF?

REPLACE function replaces a particular string with the specified string in all occurrences.

Syntax:

REPLACE (**SourceString**,**StringToReplace**,**StringTobeReplaced**)

Example:

SELECT REPLACE ('Hello world','l','d')

Output:

Note:

All the occurrence of character 'l' will be replaced by character 'd' from 'Hello world' string. We cannot replace character within the from-to positions.

STUFF function deletes a specified length of characters and inserts another set of characters at a specified starting position.

Syntax:

STUFF(**String**, **Starting Position** , **length** , **New String**)

Example:

SELECT STUFF('Hello world', 1 , 2 , 'Happy')

Output:

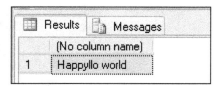

Note:

Here, only the two characters 'He' will be replaced with 'Happy' and the output is 'Happyllo world'.

50.   NEWID versus NEWSEQUENTIALID?

- ➢ NEWID() and NEWSEQUENTIALID() are used to generate GUID values.
- ➢ NEWID() function generates the GUID in random order.
- ➢ NEWSEQUENTIALID() generates the GUID in sequential order.
- ➢ NEWSEQUENTIALID() cannot be used in SQL queries and only used with DEFAULT clause while CREATE/ALTER table.
- ➢ NEWSEQUENTIALID() is easily predictable, so it is better to use NEWID() in case of privacy and security.
- ➢ To generate GUID in query, use NEWID() function

Example:

```
SELECT NEWID()
```

Output:

Example:

```
Create table #SampleSeqID

(

Id1 uniqueidentifier default NewID(),

Id2 uniqueidentifier default NewSequentialID()

)

Insert into #SampleSeqID default values

Insert into #SampleSeqID default values

Insert into #SampleSeqID default values

Insert into #SampleSeqID default values

Insert into #SampleSeqID default values

Insert into #SampleSeqID default values

SELECT * FROM #SampleSeqID
```

Output:

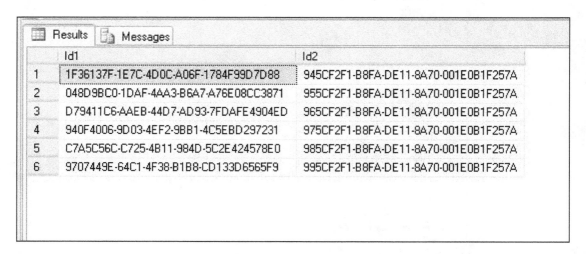

	Id1	Id2
1	1F36137F-1E7C-4D0C-A06F-1784F99D7D88	945CF2F1-B8FA-DE11-8A70-001E0B1F257A
2	048D9BC0-1DAF-4AA3-B6A7-A76E08CC3871	955CF2F1-B8FA-DE11-8A70-001E0B1F257A
3	D79411C6-AAEB-44D7-AD93-7FDAFE4904ED	965CF2F1-B8FA-DE11-8A70-001E0B1F257A
4	940F4006-9D03-4EF2-9BB1-4C5EBD297231	975CF2F1-B8FA-DE11-8A70-001E0B1F257A
5	C7A5C56C-C725-4B11-984D-5C2E424578E0	985CF2F1-B8FA-DE11-8A70-001E0B1F257A
6	9707449E-64C1-4F38-B1B8-CD133D6565F9	995CF2F1-B8FA-DE11-8A70-001E0B1F257A

Here, *Id2* column values are sequential because it is using *NewSequentialID* function.

51.   How to add IDENTITY column to an existing table?

We can do this in two methods.

Example A:

```
SELECT   *   INTO Country_copy1 FROM Country

ALTER TABLE Country_copy1 ADD ID INT identity
```

The above ALTER TABLE command logs on a row-by-row basis and if the appropriate fill factor is not specified.

Example B:

```
SELECT IDENTITY (int, 1,1) AS ID,

* INTO Country_copy2 FROM Country
```

SELECT INTO with IDENTITY is better than the ALTER TABLE method, because SQL Server has to pass through the data only once and SELECT INTO uses FAST BULK LOAD API to copy the data.

52.   How to make an existing column as IDENTITY?

It is not directly possible to change a column into IDENTITY column or vice-versa using ALTER command. How SQL Server Management Studio doing is? It creates a new table with IDENTITY column and copy the record from existing table into the new table.

To create migration script, Open SQL Server Management Studio, alter the table, instead of saving click "Generate Change Script" icon.

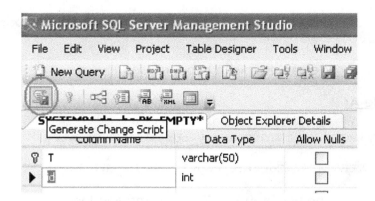

The generated script looks as below. Copy the script from the dialog box.

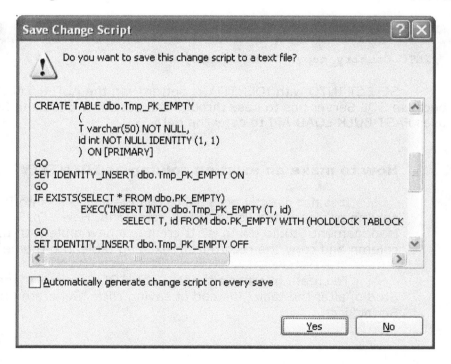

53.   How to find which table contains more records in a database?

We can find this using *sysindexes* system-table. Following query lists the table name and total-rows from the database.

Example:

```sql
USE Demo
SELECT
    object_Name (id) AS 'Table' , rowcnt AS 'Total Rows'
FROM
    sysindexes
WHERE
    indid in (1, 0) AND
    objectproperty (id, 'IsUserTable') = 1
ORDER BY
    rowcnt desc
```

Output:

	Table	Total Rows
1	BigTable	100000
2	Tbl_Sample	18
3	Employee_Salary	12
4	Employee	12
5	Labor	6
6	Users	5
7	Country	4
8	Rdbms	1
9	Identity_Test	1
10	Identity_Test2	1
11	Identity_Op	1
12	Timestamp_Demo	1
13	Log	0

54.   How to find locks?

System table *SysLockInfo* contains all the information about granted, converting and waiting locks. *SysLockInfo* table is in master database.

Example:

```
SELECT * FROM master.dbo.SysLockInfo
```

Output:

	rsc_text	rsc_bin	rsc_valblk	rsc_dbid	rsc_ind
1		0x0000000000000000000000000E000200	0x00000000000000000000000000000000	14	0
2		0x0000000000000000000000000E000200	0x00000000000000000000000000000000	14	0

55.   Ascending Index versus descending index?

While creating Index, we can specify the order of index as ascending or descending. By default it creates in ascending order.

Descending order indexes are recommended when indexed columns are used in ORDER BY clause with DESC keyword.

If the indexed column used in ORDER BY clause, SQL Server uses the index to fetch the records quickly. If a column in ORDER BY clause is descending and the index for that column is also in descending then performance will be improved. Because SQL Server no needs to go to the end of the index, it reads the descending index from its starting point.

Note:

When we query the table containing clustered index with descending order, the output records are ordered in descending order by default without any ORDER BY clause.

56.   How to use single user, multi user and restricted user mode?

By default, database works in multi user mode.

SINGLE USER

This command restricts to access only single user to the database at a time. This mode behaves as if there is an exclusive lock against the whole database.

Syntax:

```
ALTER DATABASE <DatabaseName> SET SINGLE_USER
```

Example A:

```
ALTER DATABASE Demo SET SINGLE_USER
```

(OR)

```
ALTER DATABASE Demo SET SINGLE_USER WITH ROLLBACK IMMEDIATE
```

If WITH ROLLBACK IMMEDIATE is specified, all other transactions are immediately rollbacked and disconnected and then database will be in single user mode. This will be useful when many connections are using the database and we want to close all other connections.

Output:

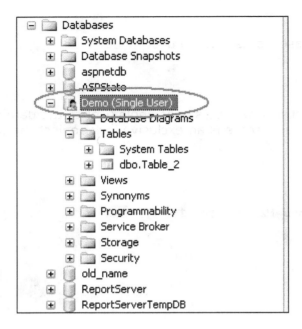

MULTI_USER

MULTI_USER mode changes back the database to default mode.

Syntax:

```
ALTER DATABASE <DatabaseName> SET MULTI_USER
```

RESTRICTED_USER

RESTRICTED_USER mode allows the database to access only to the members of *db_owner, dbcreator* and *sysadmin* roles.

Syntax:

```
ALTER DATABASE <DatabaseName> SET RESTRICTED_USER
```

Example B:

```
ALTER DATABASE Demo SET RESTRICTED_USER
```

```
Databases
    System Databases
    Database Snapshots
    aspnetdb
    ASPState
    Demo (Restricted User)
        Database Diagrams
        Tables
        Views
        Synonyms
        Programmability
        Service Broker
        Storage
        Security
    old_name
    ReportServer
    ReportServerTempDB
```

Where to use:

During upgrading or applying migration scripts in production database and we don't want any other database connections to get access, we can change the database mode into single user mode, and then do all the migrations and after completing migrations we can change the database mode back to multi user mode.

57.   Why SQL Server does not allow more than one null values for the UNIQUE column?

If you are more familiar with database designing and know the RDBMS concepts or worked in multiple database systems, then you have this hot question in your mind "Why SQL Server behaving like this in this case of UNIQUE?"

Microsoft's cool answers is "That is the behavior" and detailed response is

"We do allow one null value for a column that has a unique constraint. Having multiple null values for that column will make that column "not unique"."

But luckily SQL Server related websites giving workarounds for this problem using *triggers, check* constraint with UDF calls, etc ...

The real fact is "it is a known bug". As per RDBMS rule one NULL value is not equal to another NULL value.

Here is the error message what we get when trying to insert second null value into the UNIQUE column.

Example:

```
INSERT INTO [dbo].[Rdbms] ([name]) VALUES (null)

INSERT INTO [dbo].[Rdbms] ([name]) VALUES (null)
```

Output:

```
Messages

(1 row(s) affected)
Msg 2627, Level 14, State 1, Line 2
Violation of UNIQUE KEY constraint 'IX_Rdbms'.
Cannot insert duplicate key in object 'dbo.Rdbms'.
The statement has been terminated.
```

Here we understood, SQL Server considering NULL as a value and comparing with the existing NULL value and throwing this error and Microsoft is not accepting this as bug and answering as behavior.

Now they could not give hot fix or service pack to fix this issue because most of the people believing this as behavior.

But they could not be silent for long time. So they come with a feature called "Filtered Index" and this can only be applicable to SQL Server 2008. Using this new feature we can only set the filter criteria for *not null* values.

Example:

```
USE Demo

-- Only Applies to SQL Server 2008

Create table Table_Unique_null_Demo (column1 integer);

create unique index ix1 on Table_Unique_null_Demo where column1
is not null;
```

SQL Server 2000/2005 users should stick with workarounds only.

58.   Known and unknown things about UDFs?

> In UDF (User Defined Function), we could not execute INSERT / UPDATE / DELETE against table or views.
> Able to query UDF like views.
> Able to execute all INSERT / UPDATE / DELETE statements against the in-line UDF.
> Result-set of scalar and multi statement UDFs are read-only.
> Result-set of table valued UDF is read-only.
> UDF can be called from SELECT, WHERE and FROM clauses.
> Scalar UDF could not be used in FROM clause (example GETDATE()).
> Could not call stored procedure from UDF.
> Could not use temporary tables inside the UDF but able to use table variables.
> Could not use Nondeterministic functions inside the UDFs.

59.   SIGN verses ABS?

ABS function always returns only the positive value.

Example A:

```
USE Demo

SELECT ABS(20-10)

SELECT ABS(10-20)
```

Output:

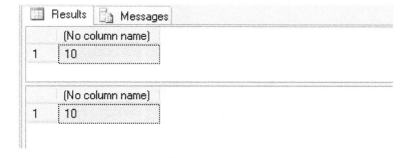

Here expression returns 10 and -10, ABS returns only 10.

SIGN function returns three possible values -1, 0 and 1. It returns -1 for negative numbers 0 for the value 0 and 1 for positive numbers.

Use this SIGN function when the decision is based on sign of the number.

Example B:

```
USE Demo
SELECT SIGN(-10)
SELECT SIGN (0)
SELECT SIGN (10)
```

Output:

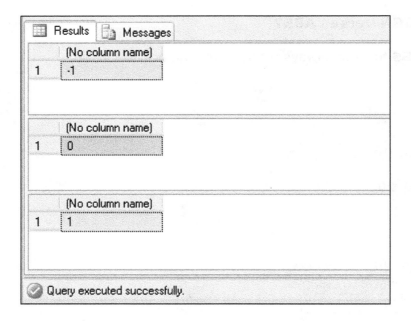

60.   How to use xp_cmdshell?
Xp_cmdshell is a system stored procedure used to execute system commands such as DOS commands from SQL Server. Due to security reason, by default the feature is not enabled in SQL Server 2005.

Example:

```
xp_cmdshell 'dir *.exe'
```

Output:

> **Messages**
>
> ```
> Msg 15281, Level 16, State 1, Procedure xp_cmdshell, Line 1
> SQL Server blocked access to procedure 'sys.xp_cmdshell'
> of component 'xp_cmdshell' because this component is
> turned off as part of the security configuration for this server.
> A system administrator can enable the use of 'xp_cmdshell'
> by using sp_configure. For more information about enabling
> 'xp_cmdshell', see "Surface Area Configuration"
>  in SQL Server Books Online.
> ```

Steps to enable xp_cmdshell

> ➢ Step #1 Launch, "SQL Server Surface Area Configuration"

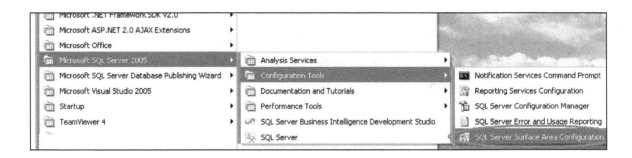

> Step #2 Click the option, "Surface Area Configuration for Features" link.

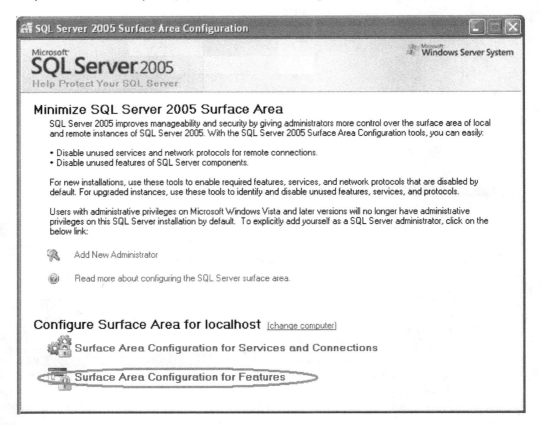

> Step #3 Select xp_cmdshell from left side pane, choose "Enable xp_cmdshell" checkbox and Click OK.

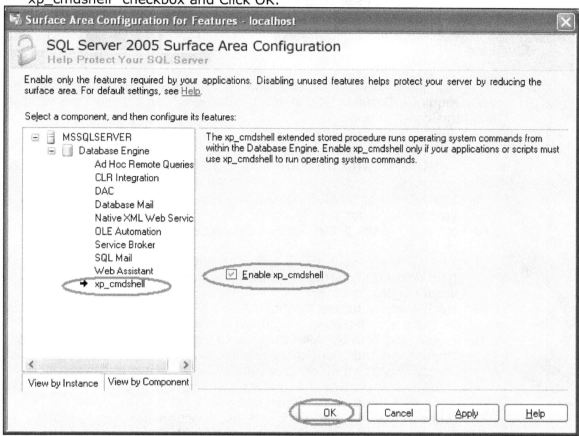

Now run the same statement again in Query Analyzer.

Output:

	output
1	Volume in drive C has no label.
2	Volume Serial Number is 7CCE-9BF5
3	NULL
4	Directory of C:\WINDOWS\system32
5	NULL
6	08/04/2004 06:26 AM 183,808 accwiz.exe
7	08/04/2004 06:26 AM 4,096 actmovie.e...
8	08/04/2004 06:26 AM 98,304 ahui.exe
9	08/04/2004 06:26 AM 44,544 alg.exe
10	09/15/2004 10:20 PM 12,498 append.exe

Now you can see DOS command result as result-set.

Caution:

Do not enable this setting in production envrionment unless this setting is really required. Becuase SQL injection attackers can damage the databse server using this command.

61. Known and unknown things about multi language data?

- Use NCHAR or NVARCHAR to store non-English language data. 'N' prefix stands for National.
- NCHAR / NVARCHAR / NTEXT data types are designed to support Unicode characters.
- VARCHAR can hold maximum up to 8000 characters but NVARCHAR can hold only 4000 characters because Unicode character need 2 bytes to store single character.
- Decide where to use NVARCHAR or VARCHAR. Do not use NVARCHAR in all the places because it occupies more space.
- Converting NVARCHAR data type column to VARCHAR cause data loss.
- Upper case and lower cases are not available in all languages so while comparing string do not use upper/lower functions.
- Date, currency, decimal formats are different in different culture, so do not split values by symbols like "/", ".", "-".
- While extracting date datatype, use functions like YEAR, MONTH and DAY
- Do not split decimal values using "." (dot). For example in Sweden currency, they separate the decimal values by "," (comma). So don't handle numbers as strings.

62. How to choose right data type?

Numeric

If you look well designed databases, you can find columns with NUMERIC data type with default precision and scale. By default NUMERIC data type occupy 9 bytes per value.

But most of the DB developers do not consider about right data type. Large data types occupy more space and also affect the performance.

For example, consider a master table *Payment_Mode* contains records like *Cash, Card, Cheque*, etc... and the *id* column is NUMERIC(9). The table can contains maximum of 10 records.

9   X 10 = 900
(Size X rows)

Here,

NUMERIC – 9 byes
Number of records - 10
So developer may think 900 bytes is not an issue.

The master table will be referenced by a trasaction table *Transactions* and the *PaymentTypeId* column using the same data type. Transaction table contains huge number of records and it may be 1000 or 10,00,000 or even more. Now if a value consumes 9 bytes to hold the *paymentId* then what is the total consumtion?

9 X 10,00,000 = 90,00,000

While desiging tables, mainly master tables, analyze what is the maximum value or how many number or records it can hold? Based on the count, choose the right data type for master table. Then Transaction tables also use the same data type for the referenced column.
In this case for *PaymentType* column TINYINT data type itself is enough and it occupies 1 byte and the rage is 0 – 255

Master table
    1 X 10 = 100
Transaction table
    1 X 10,00,000 = 10,00,000

9 times less space consumtion!

If you think, the master table contains more than 255 records, then think about SMALLINT data type and the range is -32,768 to 32,767. Even if you think it is not enough, consider INT or BIGINT datatype.
For example, columns like age, experience TINYINT is sufficient and for most of the master tables SMALLINT is sufficient.

String

Most of the people are aware of CHAR and VARCHAR. Mostly database developers use VARCHAR, it is good but in case where CHAR is the right choice, don't use the VARCHAR. For example if *EmployeeID* column values are always 10 characters length then choose CHAR datatype.

Also do not use VARCHAR(8000) and varchar(4000) for small values like name, email address, gender, etc...

Consider Small prefixed data types

> Money (8 bytes) and Smallmoney (4 bytes). Smallmoney rage is 214,748.3648 to 214,748.3647
> Datetime (8 bytes) and Smalldatetime (4 bytes). Smalldatetime rage is Jan 1, 1900, to June 6, 2079
> In SQL Server 2008 new data types used to hold only date or time. Use this datatype to store Date of Birth, Date of Join, etc...

Bollean

If a table contains 1 BIT column, it occupies one byte and upto 8 BIT columns it use only one byte. If a table contains more than 8 BIT columns, then two bytes will be used. BIT data type is designed to share a single byte to hold upto 8 column values.

63.   EXCEPT Vs. NOT IN

EXCEPT returns any distinct values from the left query that are not found in right query. The syntax of EXCEPT is similar to UNION. Add the EXCEPT keyword between two queries.

> EXCEPT works in the same way how NOT IN works.
> EXCEPT and NOT IN use the same execution plan

Differences

> NOT IN can compare one column but EXCEPT compares entire row.
> EXCEPT returns only distinct records.
> EXCEPT keyword is newly added in SQL Server 2005.
> NOT IN is an ANSI standard and EXCEPT is a T-SQL standard.
> For EXCEPT all the rules are similar to UNION, In SELECT clause number of columns should be equal and data types of columns are same or compatible.
> SELECT clause should not contain columns with the data type TEXT, NTEXT and IMAGE, because EXCEPT will perform DISTINCT operation and these data types could not be compared.

Example:

```
-- EXCEPT

USE Demo

(

SELECT [code] ,[name]  FROM [dbo].[Country]

UNION ALL

SELECT [code] ,[name] FROM [dbo].[Country]

)

EXCEPT

     SELECT [code] ,[name] FROM [dbo].[Country] WHERE code =
'in'

-- NOT IN


SELECT * FROM

{

SELECT [code] ,[name]  FROM [dbo].[Country] UNION ALL SELECT
[code],[name] FROM [dbo].[Country]

} AS C

WHERE C.code NOT IN ( SELECT [code] FROM [dbo].[Country] WHERE
code = 'in')
```

Output:

64.   INTERSECT Vs. INNER JOIN

INTERSECT works in the same way how INNER JOIN works. It executes two queries and returns only rows which are common in both result sets. The syntax of INTERSECT is similar to UNION. Add the INTERSECT keyword between two queries.

Differences

- ➢ INNER JOIN can compare one column but INTERSECT compares entire row.
- ➢ INTERSECT returns only distinct records.
- ➢ INTERSECT keyword is newly added in SQL Server 2005.
- ➢ INNER JOIN does not perform distinct operation.

> For INTERSECT all the rules are similar to UNION. In SELECT clause number of columns should be equal and data types of columns are same or compatible.
> SELECT clause should not contain columns with the data type TEXT, NTEXT and IMAGE, because INTERSECT will perform DISTINCT operation and these data types could not be compared.

65.   How to improve the performance of reports?

> Do not use the same copy of production database for Report. Backup and restore the production database periodically to the database which is used by report though schedule jobs.
> Use table hints in query.
> Use indexed views.
> If necessary create additional indexes.
> Reports do not perform any data modification, so make the database as read-only. [Reference: Solution 25]

66.   How to avoid dead locks?

The things you may know

> Do not increase command/query timeout duration, make it shorter
> Make the transaction block shorter.
> Do not place any time consuming queries inside the transaction block unless transaction is necessary for those queries.
> Use the appropriate isolation level based on the requirement
> While accessing the database objects from application or stored procedures access in the same order.

The things you should know

> While selecting records always use the table hints such as NOLOCK, READPAST.
> Avoid using locks. Use the new isolation level, SNAPSHOT ISOLATION introduced in SQL Server 2005. This isolation level does not make any locks on records. It maintains row version and compare the buffered row before updating the new changes. If the original record is different than the buffered record then SQL Server does not allow the update.
> Use the new features such as bulk insert and bulk update.

Also read the server time out solution [Reference: Solution 13]

67.   How to use OUTPUT clause?

OUTPUT clause is used with INSERT, UPDATE or DELETE statement, to get the rows which are affected. The results of the OUTPUT clause can be inserted into a table or temporary table or table variable.

Example:

Following stored procedure insert the deleted record into another table *User_Audit* using OUTPUT clause.

```
USE DEMO

CREATE PROCEDURE Delete_User  @userName VARCHAR(25)
AS
-- OUTPUT clause into Table with DELETE statement

DELETE FROM Users
OUTPUT deleted.id, deleted.userName, deleted.password INTO User_Audit
WHERE userName= @userName

GO

EXEC Delete_User 'John' -- Deleting user

GO

SELECT * FROM User_Audit -- It shows the delted user
```

Output:

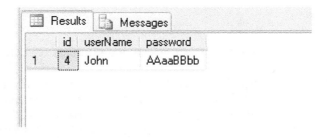

	id	userName	password
1	4	John	AAaaBBbb

68.   How to apply OOPS in SQL Server?

Database systems are classified as RDBMS and DBMS. Programming languages are classified as object oriented and procedure oriented. Inheritance is the most popular feature of OOPS and it enables reusability.

This solution will help to implement OOPS concepts in SQL Server.

User Defined Functions (UDF)

If we want to enclose some business logic or calculation or formatting then create the logic as UDF and call where ever it is needed. UDF can also work based on the argument passed. If we want to change the business logic, just change it in the UDF. It will get reflect in all the places where UDF is used.

UDF lead to reusability of OOPS.

VIEW

When we analyze many stored procedures, we can see much more joins and similar kind of WHERE clause conditions in many places.
Instead of adding similar kind of JOIN and WHERE clauses in many places, we can create view with the JOIN and WHERE clause conditions and use the VIEW in all the places. We can also create VIEW based on another VIEW. Up to 32 nested level views are supported.

VIEW lead to inheritance of OOPS.

Note

While using VIEW, we may encounter some issues like, any changes made in the base table do not reflect in the VIEW, until we ALTER the VIEW. Because VIEW is a logical table, it stores only the metadata. The metadata should be updated. To update the VIEWS use the system stored procedure *sp_refreshview.*

Syntax

```
sp_refreshview <viewname>
```

Example

```
sp_refreshview ' vw_Country'
```

69.   What is SQL injection attack?

If you are aware of security and hacking then you should be familiar with the term "SQL injection" attack. This is the most dangerous attack and the attackers can target any database system.

Attacker can inject vulnerable SQL statements into the database system, bypassing the front-end application. Front-end application may be desktop or web application. Mostly websites are targeted by SQL injection attackers. Public facing websites should be protected against SQL injection attack.

Attacker can able to damage the database, steal the data from database, bypass login, access the restricted data and even damage the server too.

Example for SQL injection attack

Front-end application may be developed using C# / VB.Net / Java / anything and it contains code like

```
sqlQuery = "SELECT * FROM Users WHERE userName = '" + name + "'";
```

Assume we get input value of the variable *name* is "Dame", and then the *sqlQuery* value will be like this.

```
SELECT * FROM Users WHERE userName = 'Dame'
```

If the user input is '; DELETE FROM USERS; --

Then the *sqlQuery* SQL statement created will be

```
SELECT * FROM Users WHERE userName = ''; DELETE FROM USERS; --'
```

Here single quotes (') is used to terminate the query and SQL comment (--) is used to comment the remaining query.

This is how the vulnerable SQL statements are injected just using a single quotes ('). If the statement gets executed, all the records of the table *users* will be deleted. Attacker can do anything, so beware of SQL injection attack. Read the next solution to know how to prevent SQL injection attacks.

70. How to prevent from SQL injection attack?

1. Find which user account is used by front-end application to connects to SQL Server and make sure the account should not be an administrator account and should have less privileged.
2. Disable SP_CMDSHELL feature *[Reference: Solution 60]*
3. If the application using in-line queries then always use parameter object and avoid using dynamic queries.
4. Avoid using the in-line queries in the front-end applications. Make sure the application should always access the data only through the stored procedures.
5. Restrict the user account only to access the necessary database.
6. Avoid using dynamic queries in the stored procedure.
7. Use any one of the method a or b
   a. Grant read-only permission on all TABLES and VIEWS. All the INSERT/UPDATE/DELETE operations should be done only by the stored procedures. Grant execute permission only to the necessary stored procedures.(explained below)
   b. Revoke complete read and write permission on all the TABLES and VIEWS. All the SELECT/INSERT/UPDATE/DELETE operations should be done only by the stored procedures. Grant execute permission only to the necessary stored procedures. (explained below)

Step #1 Open the database user properties.

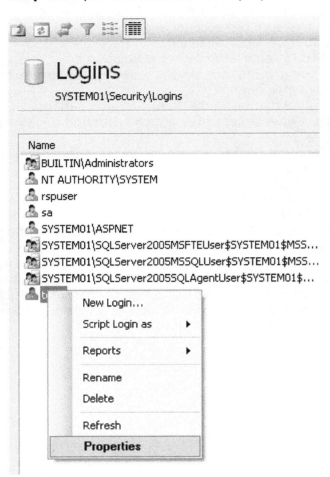

Step #2 Go to Server Roles and choose *public* in the right side pane.

Step #3 Go to user mapping, choose necessary database and role as *db_datareader* and *public.*

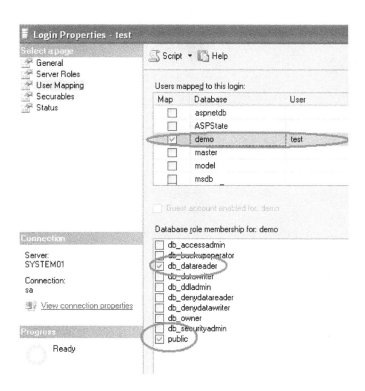

Step #4 Open Stored Procedure properties and grant execute permission to the necessary stored procedures.

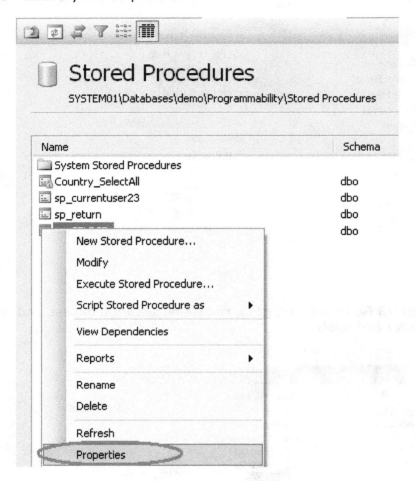

Step #5 Go to Permissions and click Add button to add the "Users or Roles", in the following dialog box browse and add the users (example *test*).

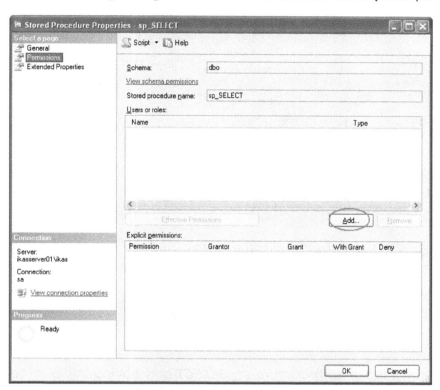

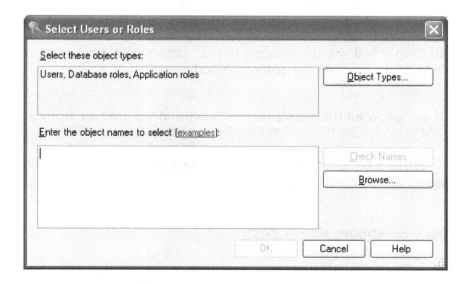

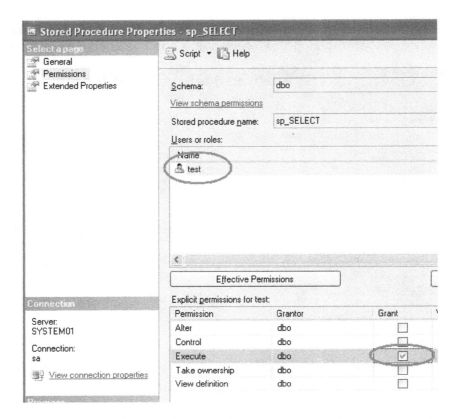

Now the stored procedure *sp_SELECT* only having the execute permission. So *test* user can execute the stored procedure. This stored procedure can contain any INSERT/UPDATE/DELETE. No other in-line queries or dynamic queries which contain INSERT/UPDATE/DELETE outside the stored procedure will not execute under the *test* user account.

In Step #4, if we not selected the *db_datareader* role we cannot even SELECT the tables outside the stored procedures.

If we follow all the above recommendation we are free from SQL injection attacks. At least follow the above first five points.

71.   How SQL Server 2005 behaves when the row size exceeds 8060?

Why the row's maximum size is 8060

SQL Server internally stores rows in the data pages. Each data page size is 8 KB (8192 bytes). One or more rows can store on a single data page. But a single row cannot span on multiple data pages. In 8192 bytes, 132 bytes are used for the internal use and the remaining 8060 (8192 - 132) bytes are used to store data.

The large data types such as TEXT, NTEXT, IMAGE, VARCHAR(MAX) and NVARCHAR(MAX) are stored on large object area and not on the main data page. These data types can support up to 2GB.

Before SQL Server 2005

For example, If we try to create a table with two VARCHAR(8000) columns, SQL Server throws warning message like there will be a possible data loss due to exceed of the maximum row size 8060. Because the sum of the total column's data type length, should not exceed 8060 bytes. If we try to insert record size more than 8060 bytes then SQL Server throws an error.

After SQL Server 2005

SQL Server 2005 does not throw any warning or error. When the total row size exceeds the 8060 bytes, then it automatically moves the data into the large object area. This new feature is known as Row-overflow.

72.   How to get the list of databases the user have access?

To list only the allowed databases

SQL Server Management studio itself lists all the databases even the connected user does not have permission. This query returns only the databases which are accessible by user.

Example:

```
SELECT name FROM sys.databases WHERE has_dbaccess(name) = 1 AND
source_database_id IS NULL  ORDER BY name
```

Output:

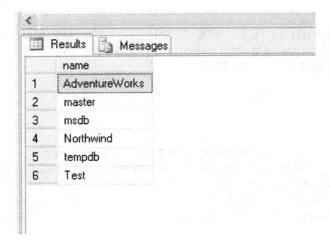

To list all databases

Sp databases

This system stored procedure lists the entire database name with size.

Example:

```
sp_databases
```

Output:

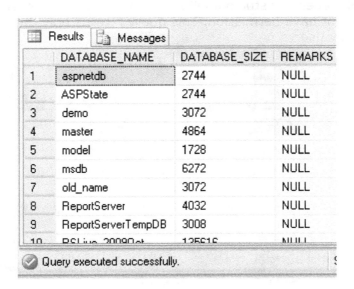

Sp_Helpdb

This system stored procedure list all the database name with additional details such as size, dbid, owner, created date, status and the compatibility level

Example:

```
sp_helpdb
```

Output:

	name	db_size	owner	dbid	created	status	compatibilit
1	aspnetdb	2.68 MB	sa	8	Dec 28 2009	Status=ONLINE, Updateability=R…	90
2	ASPState	2.68 MB	sa	9	Dec 30 2009	Status=ONLINE, Updateability=R…	90
3	demo	3.00 MB	sa	14	Mar 2 2010	Status=ONLINE, Updateability=R…	90
4	master	4.75 MB	sa	1	Apr 8 2003	Status=ONLINE, Updateability=R…	90
5	model	1.69 MB	sa	3	Apr 8 2003	Status=ONLINE, Updateability=R…	90
6	msdb	6.13 MB	sa	4	Oct 14 2005	Status=ONLINE, Updateability=R…	90
7	old_name	3.00 MB	sa	13	Feb 13 2010	Status=ONLINE, Updateability=R…	90
8	ReportServer	3.94 MB	SYST…	5	Nov 11 2009	Status=ONLINE, Updateability=R…	90

73.   How to create data script?

Microsoft SQL Server Database Publishing Wizard 1.1 is a free tool from Microsoft and it is used to generate script for data and schema.

To create data script, run the wizard. Choose the database and select necessary tables, the Wizard will create script file. Another main purpose of this tool is to publish schema and data directly to shared hosted SQL servers which cannot be accessed through SQL Server Management Studio.

Follow the steps to generate script.

Step #1 Download and install "Microsoft SQL Server Database Publishing Wizard 1.1" from
http://www.microsoft.com/downloads/details.aspx?FamilyId=56E5B1C5-BF17-42E0-A410-371A838E570A&displaylang=en

Step #2 Launch the Database Publishing Wizard from Windows Start menu and click next in the welcome screen.

Step #3 Give the server name and authentication information and click next.

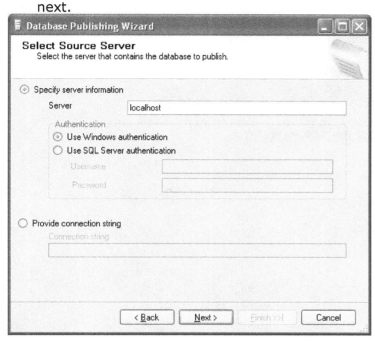

Step #4 Select the database and click next.

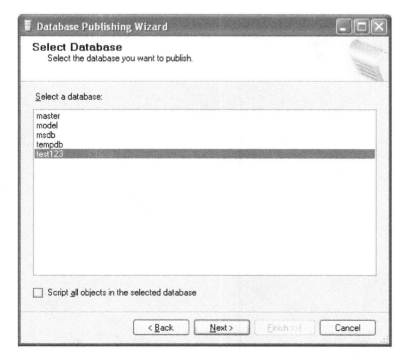

Step #5 Select the object type and click next. (To create data script, selects only Tables).

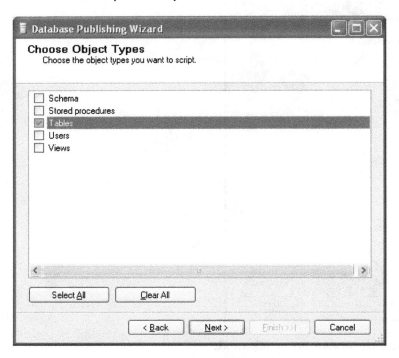

Step #6 Select the necessary tables and click next.

Step #7 Give the data script file name and click next.

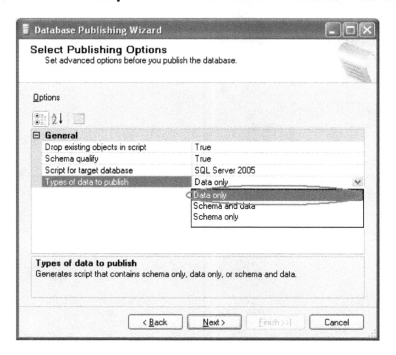

Step #8 To create data alone select "Data only" and click next.

Step #9 Reviews the summary and click next.

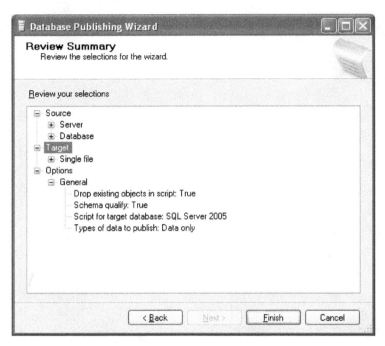

Step #10 Click close to get the generated script.

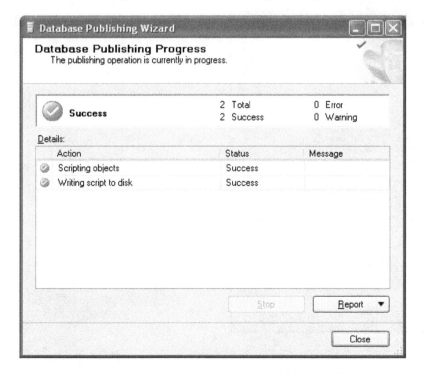

Note:

SQL Server 2008 has the built-in feature to create data script. So SQL Server 2008 users can use "Generate Script" option.

74. How to recompile database objects?

sp_recompile system stored procedure marks database objects for recompilation when the objects get called, SQL Server recompiles the database object.

Parameters of *sp_recompile* can be any database object name, if parameter is a table name then all the dependent objects such as stored procedures, triggers and views will be automatically recompiled during next execution.

Syntax:

```
sp_recompile '<<Database object name>>'
```

Example:

```
Use Demo

sp_recompile 'Employee'
```

Output:

```
Messages
Object 'Employee' was successfully marked for recompilation.
```

Where to use:

Existing statistics are invalid, if the table design gets changed. During this situation recompilation is necessary.

75.   How to implement database server-side paging?

In this following example, database server-side paging is implemented using CTE (Common Table Expression) and *row_number()* function which are the new features of SQL Server 2005.

Stored procedure *GetEmployees* only returns records based on the parameter passed.

@from N– Returns from the Nth record

@size N – Returns N number of records

Example:

```
Use Demo

GO

CREATE PROCEDURE GetEmployees @from INT, @size INT

AS

WITH Emp AS -- Emp is the name for the CTE expression

(

SELECT row_number() OVER(ORDER BY lastname )  SNO,     Lastname
FROM Employee

)



SELECT * FROM Emp

WHERE SNO >= @from AND SNO < @from  + @size - Condition to only
return paged records

GO
```

Here the records are ordered by *lastname* column using OVER and *row_number()* function. *row_number()* returns the sequential number.*SNO* column represents the sequential number which is filtered by the parameter *@from*, so query returns records only for requested records.

Example:

```
GetEmployees 1, 5
```

Output:

1 to 5 records are returned.

Example:

```
GetEmployees 6, 5
```

Output:

Next 5 records from 6th record are returned.

Example:

```
GetEmployees 11, 5
```

Output:

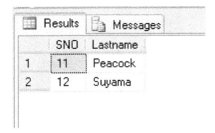

Total records are 12 so SP returns only 2 records instead of 5 records.

What is database server-side paging?

In real world web application, mostly records are displayed in page by page example Google. Instead of returning all queried-result, server-side paging method returns only set of records as page by page.

For example *Employee* table contains 5000 or more records. Front-end application displays only 10 records at a time. In this case instead of sending 5000 records to front-end application, server-side paging method makes the query to return only 10 records. Database server-side paging improves the performance by reducing the network traffic.

76. How to convert result-set to comma-separated string without loop?

We can do this using simple assignment operator.

Syntax

```
SELECT <@Variable1> = <@Variable1> + <Columne1> + ',' FROM
<Table>
```

Example

```
DECLARE @names VARCHAR(4000) -- Declare variable

SET @names = '' -- Setting initial value

SELECT @names = @names + [name] + ',' FROM Country -- name
column values appended to variable @name

SELECT @names AS Names -- Returning to final value
```

Output

77.   How to convert comma-separated string to result-set without loop?

We can do this using new xml features. First we have to convert the comma-separated string into xml type then using xml built-in function *value* extract items as result-set.

Example

```
DECLARE @data VARCHAR(MAX), @delimiter VARCHAR(5)

SET @data = 'India,Sri Lanka,United Kingdom,United States' --
input

SET @delimiter = ',' -- Here deliminater is ,

DECLARE @textXML XML; -- Declaring xml type

SELECT @textXML = CAST('<item>' + REPLACE(@data, @delimiter,
'</item><item>') + '</item>' AS XML); -- Replace (,) with
</tem><item> and make it as xml

SELECT T.field.value('.','VARCHAR(8000)') Item FROM
@textXML.nodes('/item') T (field) -- Using xml butilt-in function
VALUE, extracting each values of xml
```

<u>Output</u>

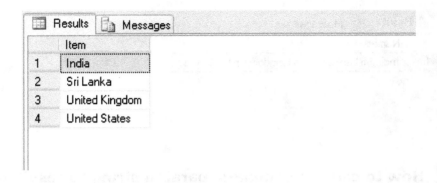

SQL Server 2005 Vs. 2008

The points which are marked below as **bold** are version changes

Database Engine object	SQL Server 2005	SQL Server 2008
Batch size	65,536 * Network Packet Size	65,536 * Network Packet Size
Bytes per short string column	8,000	8,000
Bytes per GROUP BY, ORDER BY	8,060	8,060
Bytes per index key	900	900
Bytes per foreign key	900	900
Bytes per primary key	900	900
Bytes per row	8,060	8,060
Bytes in source text of a stored procedure	Lesser of batch size or 250 MB	Lesser of batch size or 250 MB
Bytes per VARCHAR(max), VARBINARY(max), xml, text, or image column	2^31-1	2^31-1
Characters per NTEXT or NVARCHAR(max) column	2^30-1	2^30-1
Clustered indexes per table	1	1
Columns in GROUP BY, ORDER BY	Limited only by number of bytes	Limited only by number of bytes
Columns or expressions in a GROUP BY WITH CUBE or WITH ROLLUP statement	10	10
Columns per index key	16	16
Columns per foreign key	16	16
Columns per primary key	16	16

Columns per nonwide table	1,024	1,024
Columns per wide table	30,000	30,000
Columns per SELECT statement	4,096	4,096
Columns per INSERT statement	**1024**	**4096**
Connections per client	Maximum value of configured connections	Maximum value of configured connections
Database size	524,272 terabytes	524,272 terabytes
Databases per instance of SQL Server	32,767	32,767
Filegroups per database	32,767	32,767
Files per database	32,767	32,767
File size (data)	16 terabytes	16 terabytes
File size (log)	2 terabytes	2 terabytes
Foreign key table references per table4	253	253
Identifier length (in characters)	128	128
Length of a string containing SQL statements (batch size)1	65,536 * Network packet size	65,536 * Network packet size
Locks per connection	Maximum locks per server	Maximum locks per server
Locks per instance of SQL Server5	Up to 2,147,483,647	Limited only by memory
Nested stored procedure levels6	32	32
Nested sub queries	32	32
Nested trigger levels	32	32

Non clustered indexes per table	259	999
Number of distinct expressions in the GROUP BY clause when any of the following are present: CUBE, ROLLUP, GROUPING SETS, WITH CUBE, WITH ROLLUP	32	32
Number of grouping sets generated by operators in the GROUP BY clause	4,096	4,096
Parameters per stored procedure	2,100	2,100
Parameters per user-defined function	2,100	2,100
REFERENCES per table	253	253
Rows per table	Limited by available storage	Limited by available storage
Tables per database3	Limited by number of objects in a database	Limited by number of objects in a database
Partitions per partitioned table or index	1,000	1,000
Statistics on non-indexed columns	**2,000**	**30,000**
Tables per SELECT statement	**256**	**Limited only by available resources**
Triggers per table3	Limited by number of objects in a database	Limited by number of objects in a database
Columns per UPDATE statement (Wide Tables)	4096	4096
User connections	32,767	32,767
XML indexes	249	249

All the specifications are same for SQL Server 32 and 64 bit editions other than the following specification.

Database Engine object	32 bit	64 bit
Locks per instance of SQL Server	Up to 2,147,483,647	Limited only by memory
Instances per computer	50 instances on a stand-alone server for all SQL Server editions except for Workgroup. Workgroup supports a maximum of 16 instances per computer. SQL Server supports 25 instances on a failover cluster.	50 instances on a stand-alone server. 25 instances on a failover cluster.

Authors

Vijayan J

When he started his career, there were so many technologies in market, but the one he got is SQL Server. His love for SQL Server is evident from his blog http://DBExpert.wordpress.com which was his first attempt to express his thoughts to the world. By having discussions with many SQL experts, he realizes that there are so many things have to be done to become an expertise, so he did lot of experiments to become an expert. He is also a Microsoft Certified Technology Specialist in SQL Server 2005. You can keep in touch with him in twitter @VijayanJ

MK.Krizh

He is having more than 8 years of experience in software development in Microsoft platform. He is working from SQL Server 7.0 to SQL Server 2008. He is specialist in database designing, performance tuning and database security. He is happy to share his experience with you in this book.

Resource

You can download examples used in this book from www.Ranksheet.com

After download the zip file, follow the Readme.txt to setup the database and execute the examples.

Direct url http://www.ranksheet.com/Books/sql/